CLASS

What It Is
&
How to Acquire It

CLASS

What It Is

&

How to Acquire It

by

Mortimer Levitt

Atheneum · New York
1·9·8·4

LIBRARY OF CONGRESS CATALOGING IN PUBLICATION DATA
Levitt, Mortimer, ———
  Class, what it is and how to acquire it.

  1. Etiquette.   2. Conduct of life.   3. Success.
I. Title.
BJ1853.L8   1984   395   84-45127
ISBN 0-689-11415-X

Copyright © 1984 by Mortimer Levitt
All rights reserved
Published simultaneously in Canada
by McClelland and Stewart Ltd.
Composition by Maryland Linotype Composition Co.,
Baltimore, Maryland
Printed and bound by Fairfield Graphics,
Fairfield, Pennsylvania
Designed by Mary Ahern
First printing June 1984
Second printing August 1984

This book is dedicated to those few fortunate "tens" who, by their very existence, make the rest of us understand just how really exciting the gift of life can be.

ACKNOWLEDGMENTS

I want to express my appreciation to: Betty Vaughn, for her many suggestions; Gloria Stevens, for her persistence in creating order out of chaos; those friends who took time out to send me a definition of class; and, of course, to my wife, Mimi, whose serious attention is reflected in the finished manuscript.

Contents

1

Toward a Definition
of Class

To BEGIN WITH, anyone who really has class would never think of it that way and certainly never in terms of being classy. However, because class is the vernacular for that elusive quality we all admire and most of us aspire to possess, that is the way it is referred to for the most part.

In practical terms, then, what might class consist of? As I see it, there are four basic components:

1. What you say
2. How you say what you say
3. How you look
4. What you do

I prepared a preliminary list of items in each of the four categories, and it is interesting that the list on "what you do" is twice as long as the other three categories put together. And why not—what you do is the substance of class; how you do it is the style.

That, then, presents the question Can class be achieved? My good friend, Dorothy Cullman, a much-traveled woman, and sometime producer for Broadway and television, says emphatically, No.

> For me, class cannot be bought or acquired. It is an
> inner quality found without regard to financial status
> or family background. I think its essential quality is
> integrity, intelligence, and lack of pretension.
> Education can expand the horizon of a person with
> so-called class, but it will not give class to someone
> born without it. It is a state of grace that few
> people have.

I think Dorothy's general position is sound, but I disagree with her on the point that one must somehow have class from the beginning or not at all.

I happen to be a high-school dropout, born on the wrong side of the tracks and certainly without the appurtenances of class as it is usually understood. One of the many that I lacked was a middle name, having been born simply Mortimer Levitt. Being quick on the draw, I adopted the middle name of Harold. I was fourteen, and moved in one gigantic step from Mortimer Levitt to Mortimer H. Levitt. It happened that Mrs. Wrightman, a close friend of my mother, gave her the top part of a bathing suit her son had outgrown. (In those days men were never topless at the beach.) The top was emblazoned with a crimson H. I didn't know the H stood for Harvard. I assumed it stood for Harold, the name of Mrs. Wrightman's son, and claimed it as my middle initial, a claim no one bothered to challenge.

Many, many years later, having acquired other and more important appurtenances, I felt sufficiently secure to drop Harold and become, once again, Mortimer Levitt.

Although I lacked the appurtenances, I did have something that was my very own—a sense of self. I knew that I was not like the people my family grew up with. I knew that I was not born to live and die in Brooklyn. I had a hunger for something else without being sure what that something else was. I too undoubtedly confused class with its appurtenances, not realizing that my own sense of self was indeed a beginning. But I certainly did lack the appurtenances. Despite that lack, I was fortunate to have married two extraordinary women, who made me understand their significance.

I never had a relationship with anyone I respected until I met Anna, my first wife. Sad, isn't it? I was thirty. Anna lived in a completely different world from the one I knew. We met in 1936, married in 1937, and divorced in 1939—a pleasant divorce—and continued to be friends. Anna came from the right side of the tracks, blessed with both wealth and intellect. And what was it that made me attractive to her? In 1937 I was no overachiever, far from it, being a salesman at N. Erlanger-Blumgart & Co., a textile firm. What did this handsome, well-bred woman see in me? Actually, there were two things. The most important one, I suppose, is that I told the truth as I saw it, with a candor that bordered on the outrageous. There never was any question about where I stood or where I was coming from. And, yes, there was that other ingredient for which there is no rational explanation—chemistry. Anna thought I was the sweetest smelling man she had ever known. An aptitude for clothes was something I evidently was born with, in the same way that Babe Ruth, Mozart, Chris Evert Lloyd, and Charles Chaplin were born with aptitudes that, in their respective cases, made them world-famous. You can't really be a champion unless you have an aptitude to begin with. In my case, an aptitude for clothes would eventually become a career and a means for achieving a fortune.

When I met Anna, I became involved with people who were brighter and more sophisticated than the people I had grown up with. In the beginning, I was certainly self-conscious, despite my unshakable sense of self. Nevertheless, it was (and still is) totally impossible for me to say yes to anything or anyone if I disagree. But I did watch how those new people behaved, and I listened carefully.

Mimi is my second wife. Her intellect, sophistication, and generosity of spirit opened my eyes to additional aspects of living. Among other things, Mimi can transform almost anything into an event—Halloween, Easter, Christmas, anniversaries, birthdays, election day, etc. Mimi does not engage caterers or professional creators of ambiance; she uses her imagination and sense of appropriateness to create get-togethers that bring pleasure and warmth to everyone who knows us. I thought I was the easiest man in the world to live with until Mimi and I married. It was only after we were married that Mimi really came into focus. In seeing her for what she was, I was able to see for the first time my own shortcomings. At this point I would rather not offer any substantive examples of her virtues and my faults other than to say I recognize them both for what they are. And, certainly, I recognize the significant contributions both Anna and Mimi made toward my education.

The premise of this book is that class can be achieved, at least to a degree, and I will offer practical suggestions toward that end. But at this point the operative question may well be, can class be *defined?* To that question I received a wide range of responses from the friends I consulted. As they are all individuals of considerable achievement and experience, I think you may agree that their comments, as diverse and, often, divergent from one another as they appear, will help us shape a reasonably precise working definition of the term. Let us see. . . .

William Bernbach, chairman and founder,
Doyle Dane Bernbach:

> Class is unostentatious quality. It is restraint. It is modesty, an elegance of behavior, a willingness to let time measure your performance rather than a strident, meretricious "selling" of your personal wares. Class is a quiet pursuit of excellence that abhors all pretension.

Robert Ludlum, author:

> "Class" is not something I dwell on, but trust it is something I recognize. In behavior and appearance, I think "class" is the impact that comes with the simplicity of understatement. That impact is almost always accompanied by a directness in conversation and a willingness to listen. I guess it boils down to a genuine regard for other people because you have the same regard for yourself.

Gerald Schoenfeld, chairman of the board,
the Shubert Theaters:

> Class is a combination of many elements which are immediately recognizable, but if asked to describe it puts one at a loss as to how to do so.

Herbert Salzman, former ambassador to the Organization for Economic Cooperation and Development in Paris:

> "He has class" is the ultimate compliment. It indicates a person with instinctive generosity; it is a spontaneous expression of a person's character. Such a person is totally unconcerned with making an impression upon others. It derives from utter personal security and usually stems from an upbringing that can afford clear standards of "what is done," but may also develop regardless of station in life (leaving aside the Sicilian Brotherhood of the Black Hand). A person may be said to have "class" who is never in doubt as to the "right" thing to do and does it instinctively. Such a person is "inner-directed" in the sense that he takes his own behavior for granted and the approval of the group is immaterial—he knows that whatever he is doing is "right" because it meets his own standards.
>
> "Style" is frequently used as a synonym for "class" because the American culture likes to think of our society as democratic, and "style" doesn't imply the historical meaning of "class." Those who voluntarily remained aboard the S.S. *Titanic* and sang "Rock of Ages" as the ship went down can truly be said to have made their exit in style, to have shown "class." Although it was the ship's orchestra who

played while the passengers sang, it is, oddly enough,
only the singers who are remembered, all of whom
were first-class passengers.

Roger Starr, editorial board,
The New York Times:
"Class" used as an adjective in the sentence, "Joe
DiMaggio has class," for example, means that the
person so described embodies the virtues of the social
class to which he belongs, or would like to belong. In
any case, it's the nobility to which everyone assumes
everyone else would like to belong, and so class is
simply a rough version of the word *noble*; it's really
the lingering remnant of what was called chivalry,
meaning the code of conduct of people able to own
horses in the medieval economy. Class, or chivalry,
involves a *style of dress*, a set of manners, and a code
of conduct that is a highly refined version of the art
of war: generosity in victory, calm in defeat,
deportment that calls attention not so much to
individual behavior but rather to conformity with
socially acceptable ideals. We assume that noble people
are immune to self-doubt, qualms, vanity, envy. Maybe
they are. I never knew any well enough to be
absolutely certain.

Elise MacLay, author:
Class is like happiness. It is acquired with casual grace
in the attainment of something else. But the something
else must be noble and the pursuit of it must be true. So
it is that Mother Theresa has class and the Duchess of

Windsor does not. Class is caring about what is eternal and not caring about what is not.

William Schuman, composer, former president,
Lincoln Center:
Class is a collective word which encompasses many things, but in the sense you are using it, it refers exclusively to style and substance. Style is characterized by a consistency of graciousness and substance by the indefinable inner qualities which supply the flesh to the style.

Manya Starr, screenwriter:
Class is what you ain't got if everybody knows it except you.

Gay Talese, author:
I always thought of class as a convincing manifestation of poise under pressure—something many of us aspire to, but rarely does the effort achieve the ideal.

William Honan, cultural news editor,
The New York Times:
Although class has many strongly positive connotations, it also brings to mind some dark thoughts. That's because originally the notion of "class" was an admiring reference to the conduct of the aristocracy. Now, of course, there never really was and there never really will be anything to admire about the way rich and privileged people behave. Generally, throughout history, they have behaved

badly. And, thus, it is an unfortunate comment on our short memories and our present shallowness that "class" has come to mean something quite positive, something we all crave to possess.

Nevertheless, we are so far removed from the worst evils of a rigidly structured class system that we forget that a century or more ago "class" was an approving term for the license, irresponsibility and spoiled-brat behavior of those who found themselves, by birth or by good luck, on top of the heap. We forget that today. We think of class as the noble bearing of Jacqueline Kennedy at her husband's funeral and we don't recognize that class was also a mark of the conduct of Edward Kennedy at Chappaquiddick. That, too, was class. Nobody but a spoiled aristocrat would have behaved as Teddy behaved then, and certainly no one else would have gotten away with only losing his driver's license; excepting perhaps a U.S. Senator with the very best legal services. So, you see, I have a good deal of trouble thinking that "class" is simply a wonderful thing to have or possess, because I remember the origin of the terms.

Edward Meyer, chairman and president,
Grey Advertising:
Class is superiority performed with grace.

Leonard A. Lauder, president, Estée Lauder:
Class is not saying what you really feel like saying all of the time.

Jack Garfein, producer and director:
Class is when you're not concerned about it.

Ruth Spears, author:
Because "class" is not a classy word, there is nothing I can say about it.

Jacob Javits, former U.S. Senator:
My definition of the word "class" is that it is synonymous with "quality." It does not mean wealth, birth, or position. It does mean that innate sensitivity to other people, that appreciation of the good, the decent, and the fair, and that hunger for the beautiful and the appropriate that distinguishes an individual as a person one can be rewarded to know. While "class" is an indefinable quality that can occur anywhere and with anyone, it is unmistakable and readily identified. It can be felt as well as perceived and it is to be treasured when it manifests itself. It does not mean that all others must be relegated to some outer darkness, but it is a joy when found and appreciated.

Judy Price, president and publisher,
Avenue magazine:
Few of the people I meet have it. Many are stylish; many, successful; some, even unique. But few have that special combination of qualities: a sense of self without egotism; a sense of worth without wealth; and a sense of style achieved with ease rather than by artifice.

William F. May, dean, Graduate School of
Business, New York University:

> A person with class possesses assurance but not
> arrogance; pride but not conceit; sympathy but not
> sycophancy—one that has a deep unpretentious
> nobility.

Skitch Henderson, composer/conductor/pianist:

> Class to me means the assimilation of culture, whether
> it be the best bricklayer, carpenter, composer, or
> conductor. With many professions there is an
> organized dress code, and, speaking as a working
> musician, well-tailored but comfortable clothes give
> me an inward class and warmth which helps my
> professional life.

Brendan Gill, author and critic,
The New Yorker:

> The adjective "classy" is an old-fashioned slang term,
> which nobody likely to be so described would ever
> employ. The highest degree of class is the least visible;
> the odds are very much against its being achieved in
> a single lifetime and certainly not through effort or a
> sedulous aping of one's betters. F.D.R. had class, but
> Eleanor Roosevelt had far more class than her husband
> did. She was at ease with all kinds of people, while he
> was at ease only with his peers; he talked down to the
> so-called lower orders, though they never seemed to
> notice. Few presidents and still fewer business

executives have class, and no wonder: scrambling for place is ruthless as well as untidy, and nice guys do tend to finish last. Scott Fitzgerald said, "I speak with the authority of failure." No self-pity, no plea for sympathy—in a word, "class."

Arvin Brown, artistic director,
Long Wharf Theater:

The man I would consider as having true class is a man who possesses an innate, honest and comfortable sense of self. One aspect of that self would be an acute sensibility which allows him his own personal and unique concept of beauty in all things. That man, for me, has class.

Vada Stanley, marketing executive:

Class is the art of being true to oneself under all circumstances and with all people. A person with class treats a charwoman the same as a duchess, or, in the manner of Henry Higgins, a duchess the same as he treats a charwoman. He doesn't toady and he doesn't bully: he doesn't condescend, nor does he fawn. No one can intimidate him. I think being gracefully unintimidate-able is the height of class.

Kenneth J. Lane, jewelry designer:

Class to me comes from the inside—from the spirit, i.e., generosity of spirit—sense of loyalty—the ability to please, to love, to give, etc. Class cannot be bought —*cannot be worn.*

Harold Proshansky, president,
The Graduate School and University Center of the
City University of New York

I have often referred to people as either having or lacking class and while I have often meant this in terms of how they look and dress, more often I have meant how they deal with a problem or a conflict. For example, people who "continually wash their dirty linen in public" lack class, and, for me, people who lie either to avoid problems or create false solutions also lack class. Even among some of the most distinguished corporate leaders of the nation—what little experience I have had with them—I am able to tell you those who have class and those who have not.

While education and money help in establishing class, I can assure you I have found it in people who lack both.

Peter Yates, producer and director:

Class is consideration for others, and manners, which, after all, are the same thing.

Edward Koch, mayor, New York City:

Class or classy is a state of mind, both in the person who is perceived as classy and the observer who makes that determination. It is a matter of distinctive style, a manner, and an outlook which demonstrate independence and solid substance, something that is worth emulation.

Molly Haskell, author:

Class has an ethical as well as an aesthetic side. That is, it implies virtue, selflessness, as well as style. It's a modish way of paying tribute to morality by people who wouldn't be caught dead using *that* old word— even before Jerry Falwell appropriated it. To attribute class to somebody is to express admiration without envy. That's rare enough these days, and as beauty is in the eye of the beholder, we hope to rise a bit in our own esteem by acknowledging "'class" in others.

Jonathan Reynolds, author and playwright:

First and foremost, I think class is morality—because it demands of the individual the most rigorous precept of all: that he be truly himself, and therefore unique. Although aware of fashion (political or sartorial), the person with class must be flexible enough to follow fashion when it complements that uniqueness and to shun it when it doesn't. However, the particular uniqueness must be admirable: several folks who live on the Bowery are decidedly unique but couldn't be considered to have class.

   Second, I think class has very little to do with birth and almost everything to do with upbringing: class is usually learned, seldom inherited. There are far too many classless aristocrats, from Princess Margaret of England to Huntington Hartford of America, and there are far too many people without genetically privileged backgrounds who do have class, from Diana Ross to Cary Grant. I think one may learn from a privileged background, but it is still learning.

And, finally, just to negate the above, class, like its opposite, kitsch, is always in the eye of the beholder: one man's Fred Astaire is another man's Sammy Davis, Jr.

Mrs. William Woodside, special consultant,
Drug and Alcohol Rehabilitation:
To get class, choose your parents wisely.

John Mack Carter, editor-in-chief,
Good Housekeeping:
Class is the act of living without compromise, hewing unfailingly to an individual and self-imposed standard of performance. Prime examples in fiction are Sidney Carton and Gunga Din, in real life Robert Moses and Jacqueline Onassis.

Sally French, banker:
Class is a human condition that occurs when one has used inherent skills to their full potential without hurting anyone else in the process. It is achieved when one has gone through adversity without becoming bitter or cynical. It is thinking of others before thinking of one's self. And, of course, class means having a collar that fits your neck.

Bernard Geis, publisher:
Plato said, "Some wisdom can't be told, only learned." That axiom is equally true of class, style, manner, or whatever one wants to call it. How might one set about learning how to acquire "class"? Emulation. The

reward is considerable. Life will promptly become more pleasant, not only for yourself but for everyone with whom you come in contact.

A. E. Hotchner, author:
Class is a unique self-quality possessed by certain people that sets them apart and incites admiration in their fellow man. It is compounded of:
- A sense of knowing who they are, where they are headed and being extremely good at what they do.
- A total lack of hostility, jealousy or envy.
- A polite consideration for the rights and talents of others.
- A controlled ambition.
- Wisdom nurtured from experience.
- A disdain of complaining, especially about fate.
- A tendency toward having good luck.

Bill Blass, designer:
Class means the Yale Class of '22.

Based upon this diversity of quotations, you may agree that it is almost impossible to say precisely what class is—in fact, it is almost easier to say what class is *not*. And, in doing that, we can, I think, usefully summarize the most significant points my friends made on the subject.

Class Is Not One Thing, But a Combination of Qualities and Attributes

For this reason it does not lend itself to easy identification. One cannot say "up to this line, no class; step over this line, pouf, class." *Therefore, we should be flexible and perhaps rate ourselves on a class scale of one to ten.* In fact, rating public figures and friends (in absentia) on a class scale might make for an amusing after-dinner game. Mimi and I found the idea so intriguing that we looked over our personal list of some 183 individuals to determine how many "10"s we could find. Although it was my opinion and the opinion of many of those who sent me quotes that 10s are rare, it was still a surprise to find that among this large list of overachievers we would give a 10 to only seventeen, after which Mimi and I decided that those seventeen names would be carried secretly to our respective graves.

Class Is Not Dependent on Birth, Background or Education

There are many examples of persons with humble beginnings who acquired class in the course of their lives. Noël Coward was raised with bedbugs. Yves Montand left school at eleven to work in a spaghetti factory, then on the docks, then as a hairdresser's apprentice, and finally as an impersonator of Donald Duck in the streets of Marseilles. Lord Olivier never had a bath in clean water as a youngster; his turn came only after his father and elder brother had bathed in the same water. Then there is Martin E. Segal, who, like me, was a high-school dropout born on the wrong side of the railroad tracks. Marty, a successful entrepreneur, is now chairman of the board of Lincoln Center, probably the world's most prestigious cultural center for the performing arts. All these men overcame their early disadvantages to emerge as individuals with extraordinary presence, personality, and character.

Actually the list could be extended because in truth it would be almost endless. Conversely, there are as many examples of persons who failed to convert their advantageous beginnings into anything approaching class. Still, such concepts as the right schools die hard, as may be seen in this report from the *Wall Street Journal* of September 29, 1982:

> Last spring, the moment of truth arrived for Christine Whelan. An envelope came from a school that, in the words of her mother, would make the difference between being "on track for Harvard" or "stuck in second-stringville for the rest of her life."

The amusing thing about this report is that the child in question was four years old and the notice was acceptance to a kindergarten!

Class Is Not Necessarily an Accoutrement of Wealth and Power

A number of my friends noted that one's social rank does not automatically confer class. One example: Since 1950, Mimi and I have been spending our summers in Westport, Connecticut. Once a week I am a commuter catching the 7:45 train at our tiny Greens Farms station. Frances Maher, the woman who sells me my round-trip, senior-citizen ticket, is so alert and personable that she makes me and all the other early-morning commuters feel good. In terms of prestige, Frances's job lacks status, yet she dominates her small world with the authority and grace of a queen. Many points on our class scale should be awarded to anyone who gives the impression of enjoying life to the extent of making others feel good. Frances Maher is that kind of person.

One friend brought up the question of old class versus new class. Old class refers to those who were born to money several generations removed whereas new class refers to people for whom social doors are being opened because of first-generation money. The mistake my friend makes is confusing perceived class with real class. While the old money people may have all the appurtenances, they frequently lack inner strength and self-respect, knowing that they live only on hand-me-downs which, in their case, refer not to clothes, but to money.

Gloria Vanderbilt's father, Reggie, son of Cornelius Vanderbilt, was one of the world's richest men in 1922 and, aside from the Prince of Wales, the world's most eligible bachelor. His death, hastened by alcoholism, came at the age of forty-seven. We are all familiar with dozens of similar tragedies in the lives of those who started life with extraordinary privileges. Unfortunately, power and wealth can not always cover up basic weaknesses. And sometimes they serve only to create the opportunity for people to expose their innate vulgarity.

Of the rich, with whom he spends most of his time, Truman Capote once said, "Take away their money and you have nothing." While this is not necessarily the case, it is, sadly, often the case. On the other hand, the Rockefeller brothers, despite their wealth and position, worked, and worked very hard.

Jimmy Wechsler, former editor-in-chief of the *New York Post*, was once invited by President Johnson to a small luncheon at the White House. After two iced teas, Wechsler excused himself from the table and asked the butler for directions to the powder room. The President got up from the table and said, "Hold on, Jimmy boy, I'll show you the way." Johnson opened the bathroom door for Wechsler (it was a "one-holer"), and said, "Come on, Jimmy, don't be shy, let's pee together."

It is possible that was class in Texas, but I believe it was more representative of LBJ than his fellow Texans.

I asked our friend Rita Salzman (she and her husband Herbert have a home in Klosters, Switzerland, and have been skiing there for many years) to send me the following anecdote about Prince Charles, illustrative of class in high places:

Surely the story must start with the Guler family and

the tiny seventeen-room hotel called the Wynegg, owned by them for three generations and the favored haunt of many members of the European aristocracy.

Until last year it had no rooms with private baths and the accommodations were simple. This shortage of luxury and privacy didn't deter the British of "good families" from coming there and probably enjoying having to walk through each other's rooms to use the facilities. The Wynegg provided a homey atmosphere, comfortable lodging and good food for the least amount of money possible. In recent years, Ruthie Guler has taken her place as owner and hostess of both the hotel and the restaurant which has for so long been a favorite meeting place of British and German young people as well as others bearing some of the proudest family names in Europe.

One of the long-time young British visitors who came to Klosters to enjoy the skiing and the atmosphere and a regular client of the Wynegg, finding that his cousin, the Prince of Wales, wanted to learn to ski, and not caring for chi-chi of St. Moritz or Gstaad, found it only natural to invite Prince Charles to Klosters where he soon became a regular visitor.

The townspeople respected his privacy. The town policeman assigned to guard him treated Prince Charles with unobtrusive courtesy, as did the owner of the sport shop who provided his ski equipment, and the village doctor who treated the inevitable pains and strains to be expected of a vigorous and courageous skier.

In the evening, when Prince Charles and his hosts would go to the Wynegg to have fondue, and Wiener-schnitzel, he and his friends might, as is the custom in

Switzerland, share a table with other guests who came there for dinner and for whom there was no other space available.

Thus, it didn't seem odd for Prince Charles to invite to his wedding those people from Klosters who had so often looked after him and with whom he had become friends. They, of course, were thrilled, and yet they were still reluctant to discuss their relationship with him. They not only attended the wedding clad in their best, but they were presented to Lady Diana. She had been thoroughly briefed by Prince Charles and not only recognized their names, but also knew their individual relationships to Charles. They attended all the functions, were made to feel at home and were treated as the friends and welcome guests that they were.

Each of these people had contributed something to the life of the Prince of Wales, had given him a measure of attention, pleasure, and affection. This was his way of thanking them. Though they had no titles either before or after their names, they had shown friendship to Charles and he to them. They were equal as friends.

Class Is Not an Adjunct of Glamor, Celebrity or Self-Promotion

The world's beautiful people and jet-setters are notorious for failing to live up to their image.

In her day Vivien Leigh was even more beautiful, if such a thing is possible, than Elizabeth Taylor, and certainly considered a better actress. Not only was she beautiful, but she was married to the handsome, urbane Laurence Olivier, one of the great actors of all time. But this made-in-heaven marriage turned out to be hell, according to published disclosures by Noël Coward and Lord Olivier. Vivien Leigh turned to alcohol and was eventually institutionalized, and this wonderful marriage between two beautiful, talented individuals ended in divorce.

Elsa Maxwell was not easy to look at. She was short and fat, with a face not unlike that of a pug terrier. Yet she was the arbiter of the international jet set in the 1940s and 1950s. The Duke and Duchess of Windsor jumped at her bidding. She knew everyone, and seemed to lead a highly glamorous life. Several years before her death, Elsa appeared nationwide on television in advertisements for Bromo Seltzer. The ads varied somewhat, but basically showed Elsa acting the hostess at fashionable parties, then saying, "That was a swell party, but I overdid it." In the final scene, Elsa swallows a Bromo and burps loudly. Down five points. Despite the fact that Elsa hobnobbed with royalty, she had no class.

Entertainment, sports and public life may provide individuals with fame, but success in these fields does not automatically confer class.

Two of America's all-time great entertainers, Judy Garland and Marilyn Monroe, died as a result of an unfortunate dependence on drugs and alcohol. Perhaps the greatest tennis player in history, Bill Tilden, made the front pages when he was arrested for molesting a young boy; so did Enrico Caruso when he was arrested for molesting a woman in Central Park. The circumstances of Nelson Rockefeller's untimely death were an embarrassment to his family, his church, and our political system.

Two of the world's most beautiful and talented actresses— Vivien Leigh and Elizabeth Taylor—started their careers high on the class scale, but their rating dropped as their careers matured.

N.Y. PUBLIC LIBRARY PICTURE COLLECTION

John F. Kennedy, one of the most glamorous and vital of all our presidents, was a legendary womanizer. Nothing more need be said about his brother Teddy than Chappaquiddick.

Increasingly, perhaps because we have become satiated with information on the unseemly private lives of famous people, there is a tendency to shrug off or even accept their peccadilloes. Many of my friends, in commenting on class, have used words like morality, ethics, decency. It's desirable not to lose sight of that facet of class, and to retain our capacity to be shocked when it is violated.

Class Is Not Style

Generally speaking, class implies integrity, compassion, a sense of fairness, plus a quality of graciousness in manner, speech, generosity of spirit, style, and image. In contrast, style refers to individuality, a unique way of doing things.

Here is one small example of style. It is an excerpt from Tracy Hotchner's novel, *Made in Heaven*, in which she describes how her father lights his cigar.

Then Papa took a cigar out of his breast pocket. I took out a match from the box on the table, waiting for him to get the cigar ready. He clipped a hole in the end with the silver folding cigar clip on his key ring, then he leaned forward for me to put the fire under it. I struck the match and let the sulfur burn off as he had taught me. I held the flame far beneath the end of the cigar so that only the heat reached the tobacco, not the flame itself. Papa slowly turned the cigar between his lips until it was evenly lit all the way around. I blew

the match out as it reached my fingers and watched
solemnly as he took the cigar out of his mouth, then
blew lightly on the end to make it glow, to be sure it
was well lit so it would burn smoothly. He nodded
his head and took an appreciative puff. I put the
matches down proudly.

It is possible to have style or class or both. For instance,
you might say that Mike Todd, producer of *Around the
World in Eighty Days*, had style when he took over
Madison Square Garden to give his then wife, Elizabeth
Taylor, a birthday party, but he might not rate very high
on our suggested class scale. And how many points would
you deduct from Elizabeth Taylor because she married
seven times?

Queen Elizabeth, on the other hand, is presumed to
have class because as a reigning monarch she has all the
appurtenances, but does she have style? I'd say no, at least
not when compared to people like the Hepburns (Katharine
and Audrey) and Kitty Carlisle Hart. They have class and
project it with style—in speech, in dress, and in behavior.

Class Is Not Lifestyle

The overused phrase usually refers to so much that it
hardly means a thing. Perhaps it is safe to say in our frame-
work that lifestyle is the behavior people exhibit and the
activities they choose for themselves during their leisure
time. To a degree, then, lifestyle may affect class, but it is
more pertinent to realize that exactly what a person does
in the evenings, on weekends, or during vacations is not

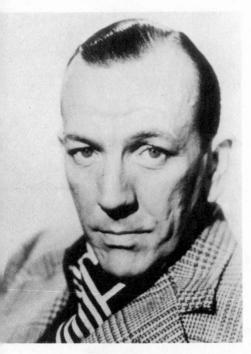

*In contrast, these three men from humble, even squalid,
surroundings rose to become universally recognized for their
high rating on the class scale—Sir Noël Coward, Cary Grant
(a stiltwalker in the circus), Lord Olivier.*

N.Y. PUBLIC LIBRARY PICTURE COLLECTION *(Cary Grant)*
WIDE WORLD PHOTOS *(Olivier/Coward)*

as important as the extent to which it is done with style.

In every society there are a modest few who have class, a few more who have style, and the balance who have only lifestyle.

Though they need not concern us greatly here, it is worth noting that there are many regional differences in lifestyle. In the Midwest leisure hours may center on grandchildren and country clubs; in California on one's tennis game and fitness; in Texas on profit opportunities for future investments; in Colorado on skiing.

Consider entertaining at home. New Yorkers invite people for dinner at 7:30, expect them to arrive at 7:45, and plan to begin dinner at 8:30. I am told that in Kansas guests are invited for dinner at 7:00, but they arrive between 6:15 and 6:30, allowing themselves the time they need for their cocktails. I was certainly surprised to hear this, and I was equally surprised on my first holiday trip to Egypt. I was there in 1945, three months after the end of the war. My hosts had a mansion on the Nile, staffed by twenty-seven servants. I was invited for dinner at 8:00; I arrived at 8:15 and learned that I wasn't really expected until 9:00 and that dinner wasn't served until 10:00. Spain is different again, because dinner is served from 10:30 to midnight. The secret to late hours in many Latin countries, of course, is the fortifying siesta taken from 2:00 to 4:00 every afternoon.

By now it must have become increasingly clear that the question of class cannot be resolved in the sense that a mathematical problem can be resolved. But it is also clear that the much admired combination of qualities and attributes that we call class really does exist and vibrantly makes its presence felt in a number of individuals. Our goal then is to enhance that quality in our own lives. I believe this can be achieved easily by schooling ourselves in what I see as the four basic components:

1. What you say
2. How you say what you say
3. How you look
4. What you do

I hope you find the suggestions in the following chapters worthwhile. In my view, acquiring some of the appurtenances of class is indeed worthwhile. It enriches one's sense of well-being, even if in a limited way, by the image one projects; the clothes one wears; the way one communicates with one's peers, the elderly, children and strangers; the gifts that one chooses; the thank-you notes that one writes; the graciousness with which one accepts a gift; what one does and how one does it. The appurtenances enrich the life of friends and acquaintances, and, even more, they enrich one's own life.

As we have only one life to live, by all means, let us enjoy it, and, shall we say, be as civilized as we can, yet true to ourselves in all circumstances.

2

---

*What You Say
and How You Say
What You Say*

ISAAC STERN, one of the world's great violinists, walked into my Fifth Avenue Custom Shop to order shirts on a day I happened to be there. With his gray pullover sweater and cap he looked like an overweight errand boy. Yet, when he began to talk, the salesperson immediately recognized his stature. Stern was a charmer, even without his violin, and there was no longer any way he could still be mistaken for an errand boy.

This chapter offers a number of simple and straightforward suggestions for practicing the gentle art of conversation, good for a point or two on your class scale rating. I'll give you three examples taken from personal experience that indicate the difficulty people have in making conversation, not only with people they don't know, but with people they know as well.

Example 1.

In my own business, consisting of fifty-nine stores, I now employ about 190 designers, people who take our customers' measurements and then advise them on how to color-coordinate shirt, suit, and necktie. Although most customers think of the Custom Shop as a shirt store, ours is actually a service business. Unlike, yet similar to, interior decorators, we are exterior decorators. Our designers, therefore, are taught not only the technical end of our business, but also how to establish a relationship in the same way that any professional person establishes a relationship with a client.

Our most difficult task is teaching trainees how to talk, how to be at ease, and how to put our customers at ease. Trainees are given a specific group of questions to help them establish such a relationship. Trainees are all college graduates, a few with graduate degrees. Yet it takes six months of nurturing to bring those trainees who successfully complete our course (only one in four) to the point of making relaxed conversation with anyone.

Example 2.

Mimi has an old friend who went to school with her in Vienna, a good-looking, well-dressed woman who was successful as a stylist for *Vogue*. Her position was to select the clothes that the models would wear in the fashion photos done at the studio of the publication, and she would dress them completely for the photographer. On one occasion she spent the night in our home. The following evening the three of us were to go first to a cocktail party at the home of a friend and then to a dinner party at someone else's home. Our friend had two drinks before we left. I said, "How can you drink now when we are going to a cocktail party and then on to a dinner party?" She said simply, "Mortimer, I am unable to face the prospect of a party unless I first fortify myself with two drinks. I am too shy, too nervous." I was shocked to learn that a woman as seemingly sophisticated as Greta could be that insecure. There had never been any outward evidence.

Example 3.

In 1942, psychoanalysts were in high repute. I went to one of the best. At one session I told him about an incident that took place at the Palm Springs Racquet Club. It was 1941, the year I retired from the day-to-day management of The Custom Shop, and I was taking a six-month automobile trip around the United States. I had been taken there by an old friend, Ben Oakland, a very successful composer of popular songs. Ben introduced me to Herbert Marshall, a handsome film star with a marvelous British accent. Marshall overwhelmed me with his graciousness. He was really too gracious. In any case, he made me acutely uncomfortable. That led me to the realization that I was also uncomfortable facing a room full of strangers. My psychoanalyst, Dr. Leonard Blumgart, was very helpful. He said, "There is no need to be uncomfortable. You are free to walk up to anyone at a party to which you have been invited, extend your hand, and say simply, 'I am Mortimer Levitt,' and take it from there." If I, as a retired millionaire at the age of thirty-four, was so unsophisticated that I required this basic advice, I might safely assume there are others who will find this chapter of more than passing interest.

Making conversation is the ability to talk easily with people you don't know as well as the people you do know—friends at a dinner party, strangers at a cocktail party, on a cruise, at a vacation resort, or whatever. On these occasions, you are not required to hold forth on the implications of William Safire's latest newspaper essay or the President's current solution for America's economic problems or the ultimate answer to the Palestinian question. These are topics that require, at the very least, a modest degree of expertise. Without that, you would, in fact, be foolish to express any opinion forcefully. Better confine yourself to asking pertinent questions. Mark Twain said it very well, "I was gratified to be able to answer promptly. I said, 'I don't know.' "

Everyone has at least one small area of expertise and most people have several. If you met Mimi in a social setting, it would be your pleasant task to uncover her special interests with a few easy questions such as "What do you do for recreation?" "How do you spend your time in the city?" and so on. Mimi can speak with authority on music, art, the problems of schools, private and public, historic preservation, history and cooking. She is a linguist and a thoroughly experienced traveler. So, if you were talking with Mimi, you would be unlikely to want for subject matter.

However, there are some questions that you should never ask. One question, it may surprise you to learn, is "What do you do for a living?" Another, "Where do you work?" Any sophisticated person would find this most offensive. Equally offensive is, "Now, Mr. Levitt, tell me all about yourself." There are more discreet ways to get the same information without giving offense. In fact, you can very quickly learn what you want to know while, at the same time, making the other person feel that you hold him in high esteem.

YOU: You're an attorney. Right? (architect, engineer, doctor, or whatever profession seems likely)

HE: What makes you think I'm an attorney?

YOU: I've known many professional men, and you have all the earmarks; you *are* a professional man, right?

HE: No, as a matter of fact, I am in business.

YOU: But you started out to be a professional man, right?

HE: No.

YOU: So, I'm wrong—it happens.

Or you may want to try this:

YOU: So, you're a career woman, right?

SHE: No, I'm a housewife.

YOU: Then you *are* a career woman. Running a home means being an administrator, social worker, psychologist, nutritionist, and maid all rolled into one. And, even more, you are responsible for maintaining the morale of the entire family. Don't you agree?

Making Introductions Easier

The first time I heard a hostess trumpeting to her assembled guests, "And now may I introduce our guest of honor, the Baron so and so . . . ," I thought it was ghastly. She made it sound like "make way for his majesty." There are ways to simplify introductions, not necessarily from the point of view of proper etiquette, but common sense introductions that make it easier for guests to have a good time in a room full of strangers. An experienced hostess will not only introduce you to other guests, but pass on a few pertinent and complimentary remarks to give you and the person to whom you are being introduced a starting place for conversation. For example: "This is my good friend, Gloria Stevens, and you had better be careful, because she's a psychologist." And, "Gloria, this is Howard Solomon, our young lawyer friend, whose star is now in the ascent," or "who has just started with CBS," or "who is going to do his best to completely change Xerox's approach to marketing."

Thus, having been given an opening by the hostess, they can then talk about their respective areas of expertise or interest.

I've been to too many parties where the hostess or host leaves a guest completely on his own. This leads to telephone calls the next day. "Oh, my God, why didn't you *tell* me that so-and-so does that." If you are giving a small party, brief your guests when they accept your invitation by telling them who else will be there. If it is to be a large

"Mr. Joseph W. Bellington. Here's what the New York 'Times' had to say about him."

Guests should be briefed about other guests beforehand and certainly upon being introduced.

party, mention the names of one or two other guests who might be of interest to that particular person.

Now, what if you have not been briefed, which is the case most of the time. You are invited to a dinner party or a cocktail party where you know no one except your host and hostess. The fact that you have been invited automatically gives you the necessary social credentials. You get your obligatory drink, and then you are on your own, faced with twenty to sixty strangers. Your hostess failed to provide any leads, but don't panic.

You may walk up to any man, woman, or couple and introduce yourself—"My name is Gloria Stevens." Your introduction will be acknowledged and returned, and now it becomes your turn to make conversation. You might try a few relevant questions along these lines. "And what is your connection with our host?" "Are you a friend of the host or hostess?" "Have you known them long?" Or, if you are on vacation, "What brings you to Jamaica?" "Do you live in the area?" "How did you decide to come here for your holiday?" "How did you decide to take this cruise?" "Is this your first cruise?" "Is this your first visit to Paris?" etc.

You can canvass the entire party using your own variations of this easy approach to making conversation. People are infinitely interesting, and the image they project seldom indicates their particular areas of expertise. That's why it is necessary to dig, not for romance, but only because people are, in fact, forever surprising.

Of course, not everything that is on your mind can be said in social conversation. For instance, it is in poor taste to ask someone's age. Cary Grant evidently thought so. When Grant was in Europe, his press agent, Clark Hedron, working on a magazine story for him, had to know Grant's age, so he sent a cable that read: HOW OLD CARY GRANT? Cary Grant wired back: FINE, HOW OLD CLARK HEDRON?

Gossip can be fun when it's gossip about famous people who'll never hear of your discussion and couldn't care less if they did. But gossip about people you know is not only morally wrong, it is also tactically wrong because it almost always gets back to the person involved.

How to Listen

Disraeli pointed out that nature saw fit to give us two ears but only one mouth. You may be perceived as charming simply because you are a good listener, letting the other person know that he or she is receiving your full attention because you really are interested. In order to be interesting, then, it is necessary to be interested, and it should not be faked.

A good conversationalist speaks to the point and listens to the points being made. He speaks in turn only when he has something to say or to draw out the person he is speaking with. If, after giving the other person a fair chance, you decide that you really are not interested, then it is easy to break away with, "Please excuse me, I need a refill" or "Please excuse me, I forgot to give our host a message," or whatever.

In the 1940s, Dorothy Thompson's syndicated political column in the *New York Herald Tribune* was second only to Walter Lippmann's column in importance. They both had an enormous readership, and their opinions were closely watched by top political figures. Dorothy's second husband, Maxim Kopf, was one of the painters I showed in my art gallery, and on several occasions I was invited to dinner at their home. To my great surprise, Dorothy Thompson turned out to be a nonstop talker. "The secret to being a successful bore," said Voltaire, "is to tell everything." Despite the fact that she was extremely knowledgeable and really very bright, Dorothy turned out to be a bore. She could talk, but she couldn't listen. She went on and on—like a waterfall. There is an old German proverb that Dorothy failed to heed: "A well-bred man makes himself out to be less than he is."

When Peter was six and Elizabeth seven and a half, our nurse began bringing the children down to meet our dinner guests during the cocktail hour. Although Peter and Elizabeth were both good-looking, happy children, I discovered that they had very little to say to our guests. After they had been down to visit on several occasions, I thought I should help them out so I told Elizabeth that I would teach her how to practice the gentle art of conversation. I wrote out a list of pertinent questions that Elizabeth might ask our guests. "Do you have any children?" "How old are they?" "Where do they go to school?" "Do they like fairy tales?" "Do they like sports?" "Have they ever been to the Museum of Modern Art?" Elizabeth was outgoing, gregarious, and seemed to be the perfect pupil. And she would ask most of the questions I had written out. Unfortunately, she seldom listened to the answers. Some years later—I think she was sixteen—Elizabeth said, "Daddy, why didn't you tell me that practicing the gentle art of conversation also meant listening to people?" Life is filled with similar misunderstandings; nevertheless, Elizabeth is now most articulate.

I have learned through considerable experience (having hosted almost a hundred dinner parties a year for the past thirty-two years) that most people have never learned to listen, and I have become increasingly impatient with people who speak before one completes a thought. When a guest

holds the floor too long and becomes boring, it is desirable
to steer the conversation to someone else. However, every
guest should be permitted to complete a thought without
interruption.

Mimi recently returned from a four-week trip to
China. At our first dinner party after her return a guest
asked Mimi sotto voce, "Tell me about your trip to China."
Mimi said, "I'll tell you in a moment; I want to hear what
John is saying." If Mimi had told her story then, our other
guests would have been denied the chance to hear it. And,
at the same time, it would have interrupted the ongoing
conversation. If our friend had thought about it at all,
she would have realized that Mimi's China story should be
heard by all the guests and not just reserved for her.

There is another kind of interrupter, who is even
worse. For example, Mimi is telling her China story and
everyone is listening; in the middle of Mimi's story, one
guest will ask another, "How is John doing at Yale?" Because a guest should have his say without interruption, I
discourage side conversations. I usually say very little,
speaking only when needed to keep the conversation interesting to everyone.

Sometimes guests are offended by the mildly autocratic
manner in which I suggest that a speaker should not be
interrupted. However, by the end of the evening, friends
are generally agreed—even though they are apt to poke fun
at me—that the evening was more enjoyable because everyone did have a chance to participate.

Handling the Inevitable Rejections

If you try to make conversation with someone who doesn't respond, it could be that at that particular time he is overwhelmed by his own problems. You cannot know, for example, that the first man you introduced yourself to had recently learned that the small spot on his back is a malignant melanoma, that the second man recently learned that his wife has taken a lover, and that the third man has reason to believe he's about to lose his job. These might be exaggerations, but life spreads its disappointments more or less evenly throughout society, and you are bound to encounter those who have recently received such a shock.

One more thing about rebuffs and unfriendly reactions. Neither you nor I nor anyone can be attractive to everyone. Someone may not respond simply because the chemistry is wrong. So move on! Look for those who find you attractive or acceptable for whatever reason.

When people come to our home for dinner and fail to return our hospitality, I don't take it personally. People have marriage problems, money problems, health problems, job problems; sometimes people are just not in a position to entertain. And, then there are those who don't want to have a continuing social relationship. Fair enough. One should not expect to win them all. Bill Cosby put it very well: "I don't know the key to success, but the key to failure is trying to please everybody."

Other Conversational Problems

Pressing one's political or moral position with excessive zeal and/or solemnity is usually a turn-off in social conversations. In any case, if you are proposing a solution to a really serious problem—crime, drug abuse, taxes, war, the subway, welfare—your message will be more palatable if you say it with a twinkle in your eye; it is a mistake to pound the message home by raising your voice, or becoming pompous. Mimi tends toward an effective use of understatement. My tendency, unfortunately, is in the other direction. Because I don't want to be misunderstood, I am apt to dot every *i* and cross every *t*. Mimi gives people room. Fortunately, I catch myself and reach for a laugh, and usually the laugh will be on me.

It is unfortunate that some guests with strong political convictions too often tend to become pedantic and overbearing. More importantly, in pursuing their point of view, they lack humor. Oscar Wilde's quip, "Seriousness is the only refuge of the shallow," would certainly be apt. To have a point of view is refreshing, but to drive it home with a sledgehammer, especially in a social situation, is undesirable. And, on such matters as politics or economics, there really is no last word. For every esteemed economist who says yes, there is another equally esteemed economist who will say no. For every esteemed politician who is a hawk, there is an equally esteemed politician who is a dove.

The Need for Humor

The brightest people I know, the really bright ones, are seldom boring. Except for Dorothy Thompson, who has passed on to her just reward, and for two others still living but better left unnamed, bright people generally do have a sense of humor; they even tell jokes. How often have you heard, "Oh, that's so funny; I wish I could remember jokes." I used to be one of those. In recent years, however, I have begun to tell jokes too—and successfully. I forced myself to do it. I'll tell you why. Sometimes I conduct classes at the Custom Shop for our management trainees, my main purpose being to teach our teachers. It is desirable to put the trainees at ease, and the easiest way to eliminate tension is to tell a joke or two.

No one can give you a sense of humor if you don't have it; however, there's nothing to prevent you from collecting a small group of jokes, jokes that you enjoyed hearing. Even though you may feel self-conscious about telling a joke, it's well worth the effort, and it's a pleasant surprise when friends laugh.

Jokes are easier to come by than anecdotes. So, whenever you hear one in good taste, write it down and edit it so you can tell it using the fewest possible words. Then practice it aloud when you're alone. It takes courage to tell a joke, if you don't have the aptitude, so you might try it out on your family or on a close friend. If you break out in a cold sweat the first few times, so what! After you get the hang of it, you'll have a new skill at making conversation.

Interestingly, I never knew that Henry Kissinger had a sense of humor. It turns out the man has two sides: the Kissinger the public sees on television is overweight, humorless, and the possessor of a most unfortunate accent. In 1982 I had the pleasure and privilege of seeing his private side; it's quite different. Friends had arranged a small dinner party in a private room at the 21 Club for Senator Jacob Javits. Kissinger was the only speaker, and he was a totally different man from the one I had been accustomed to hearing. His subject was certainly serious, mostly about the Soviet Union. He spoke extemporaneously. He was charming, witty, and knowledgeable. We saw him at his best. The public sees him at his worst. Later, Kissinger admitted to me that he is incapable of reading a speech without sounding dull.

To Drink or Not to Drink—That Is the Question

I realize that many guests need a drink to relax. However, when they have two or three drinks, they go from having nothing to say to having too much to say. Alcohol may give you a lift to begin with, but too often that lift is followed by a headache, a sudden desire for sleep, or a hangover. Therefore, our butler is told deliberately to make drinks on the light side. In contrast, a high resulting from good conversation can be sustained for an entire evening. It is not desirable to depend on alcohol. As Nancy, Lady Astor said, "I don't drink because I want to know when I'm having a good time."

When we first began entertaining, the drinking patterns were completely different. The martini was a commonplace, ditto bourbon on the rocks (newspaper people) or Scotch and soda. About fifteen years ago, friends began switching to white wine; later yet, we began getting requests for spritzers (white wine and soda), and in the past year we are getting more requests for soda only, no wine. Perrier made it fashionable. If you are a hard liquor person, you might want to try club soda or a spritzer the next time and see if you don't get more out of the evening's conversation.

Conversation in the Business World

Most of this chapter has been devoted to social occasions, but the concept of talking to people is the same for all situations, business and social. At a business luncheon, for example, it is customary to conduct a general conversation while lunching, then getting to the business reason for the lunch once you have finished eating. As the host, it is customary to ask your guest if he would like a drink before the maitre d' asks. If you are a nondrinker and your guest is a drinker, you should be gracious and order a tomato juice or Perrier so that your guest is not obliged to drink alone.

If you are a commuter and accidentally find yourself sitting next to a neighbor, a friend, or an acquaintance, it is customary to pass one or two non-involving remarks about the weather or a current sporting event, and then, almost immediately, turning to the business at hand: reading the day's newspaper, handling the unfinished work left in the briefcase, or getting back to the book you are in the middle of reading. If he or she doesn't end the conversation out of delicate regard for your sensibilities, you may close it with: "Well, it's time to read the newspaper. If I don't do it now, there's never enough time later," or something similar.

If you are an outside salesman paying a call on a client, it is desirable to make your call as personal as possible before getting down to the business at hand. You might pay a compliment on a suit, tie, shirt or suntan. Or you might make an inquiry about his family. The point is that no matter what business you are in, you are always facing competition. Therefore, the thing that differentiates you from your competitor is the image you project by the way you look, by what you say, and how you say what you say, plus, of course, your personal interest in the buyer. This is the plus you can bring to any business meeting.

At the many different kinds of board meetings (corporate, cooperative, country club, charity organization, etc.), the general behavior is, more or less, the same. Don't speak just to be heard. In other words, don't chatter. If you have a point to make, hold back if you can until the point being discussed has been exhausted. Your thinking will then reflect not only your own ideas, but any good ideas that have been suggested. You may, of course, add your voice by saying, "I believe that Mrs. Smith's point was well taken, and I am in complete agreement." A pleasantry is always in order because board meetings are too often dull.

Job Interviews

I have conducted job interviews on and off for some forty-five years, and found that the things I've read on the subject are too complicated. My advice is to keep it simple.

To begin with, walk into the office at a lively pace, indicating energy. Extend your hand and introduce yourself while shaking hands firmly: "Mr. Interviewer, my name is Mortimer Levitt, and I am delighted to have this opportunity for an interview."

Don't smoke, even if your interviewer is smoking.

Answer questions directly. If you have been fired with or without cause, this is the best time to tell the truth. It is hard to believe that one voluntarily leaves a job without first replacing it with something else.

In any case, do not leave the questioning solely to the interviewer. At tactful moments ask questions about the company. In preparation, read a copy of the annual financial report so that you can make a few comments to indicate that you did some homework before appearing for the interview. Ask the interviewer about the company's competitive situation in the market and what the company's angle is, to demonstrate entrepreneurial thinking.

The suggestions I am making should be a part of your thinking; otherwise, it may appear that you are seeking this job because it is the only offer you have. Even if that is the reason, you should in your own mind want answers to these questions so you can determine your potential for advancement within the company.

An amusing story is always in order provided it doesn't begin with "Have you heard the one about the priest, the rabbi, and the minister?"

How You Say What You Say

More often than not, it's not only what you say but how you say it that makes a difference in the degree of class you project. A modulated, expressive voice and good diction add points to your class rating. However, good diction without cordiality is indicative only of the appurtenances, not the substance, of class.

It's interesting that we never sound on tape as we do in our mind's ear. Invariably, someone who hears himself for the first time will shudder and exclaim, "Is that me? I don't sound like that." To some extent the reaction is valid. For one thing, being subjective, we hear how we intend to sound, which is often at odds with reality. If we are tense or tired, these emotional qualities are reflected in our voice and quickly picked up by others.

The disparity between how we think we sound and how we actually sound can also be attributed to the fact that we are on the inside; that is, the vibrations are in our own head, so the end result is different for someone hearing us on the outside. Then, too, if we are really involved in what we are saying, we can no more give an objective ear to our voice than we can catch the reflection of ourselves smiling spontaneously in the mirror.

The first step in improving the voice is to become aware of how it sounds by taping it. Only by being conscious of what needs changing can there be improvement.

After repeated playbacks, the adjustments to be made in the speed, volume, pitch and tonal quality will become apparent. Problems of tension resulting from tight mouth or throat muscles or from psychological factors (nervousness or lack of confidence), may require consultation with a speech therapist.

Outside help may also be required to correct faulty diction unless you have a very good ear and a lot of discipline. Bad diction is usually due to an undesirable regional accent or mispronunciation of words.

REGIONAL:	sawr	for	saw (New England)
	dis	for	this (Bronx)
	thoid	for	third (Brooklyn)

MISPRONUNCIATIONS:	agin	for	again
	jewlery	for	jewelry
	beauteeful	for	beautiful
	mischeevious	for	mischievous

Correcting these mispronunciations and regional accents requires awareness, a good ear, concentrated effort, and, above all, the desire to improve. If you have a sensitive ear, you can improve your accent by listening to talk shows on radio or television. The difference in speech between the announcer and the lay person becomes immediately evident, and it's possible to make improvements in your own speech based on the comparison.

The way in which you say something can distort its meaning. For example, "How old are you" is neutral, but "How old *are* you" is offensive.

The import of what you say can also be changed by thinking the opposite of what you are saying. I remember a receptionist who was particularly unpopular. When she was asked to do something, she usually muttered "All right" or "I'll try to fit it in." Those seemingly cooperative responses always came across as "I'm overloaded" or "This is not my job." She was totally unaware that her reluctant attitude was transmitted in her voice, unaware, that is, until I brought it to her attention. One's attitude, mental and physical state, and personality all are subtly revealed in the voice. When, for instance, we are tense, that tension will result in a voice that is high-pitched or too fast or too loud. When we are tired, fatigue will render the voice low and dull. Tension produces physiological changes in the throat and mouth muscles, which, in turn, alter the quality of the voice. We are rarely conscious of these emotional variations. This is especially evident on the telephone. When, for example, a busy worker is interrupted by the phone and forgets to switch gears, as it were, before answering, he will unintentionally project a voice-image of impatience; however, the caller hears only a disembodied voice and judges the worker accordingly. Unfortunately, on the phone your personality is judged largely by the emotional quality you project.

What is it that gives so much presence to a voice? In her book on the British class system, Jilly Cooper wrote that "pronunciation as well as the words you use are very important for determining class." In addition to diction and verbal selectivity, I would add phrasing or, to put it another way, rhythm.

The diction of today's young adults is often appalling, as is their vocabulary or lack thereof. And, because of television, we may be becoming a nation of nonreaders and possibly on the verge of becoming nontalkers as well. During the past forty-seven years almost 2,000 management trainees have been put through the Custom Shop's training program. Every applicant is given an IQ test before being interviewed, and almost ten years ago I realized that average scores had dropped a whooping 15 percent. Unfortunately, that's not all. Our trainees are taught to memorize a script on the subject of presenting an appropriate image. The script is first read aloud as one does when rehearsing a play. I was shocked to hear college graduates reading like high-school freshmen. The problem was so bad I felt obliged to hire a professional. But his approach proved much too pedantic, too complicated, and the results were disappointing. We came to a friendly parting of the ways. Subsequently, I developed a ridiculously simple approach that worked just fine. By using one easy sentence, I was able to improve poor speech patterns immediately. The sentence goes like this:

> If, I, were, to, place, an, invisible, comma,
> after, each, word, and, an, invisible, semicolon;
> after, some; words, my, speech, would, have,
> presence.

Trainees requiring help with their diction practice this sentence until the rhythm becomes natural. The improvement is almost immediate. By means of the inaudible comma, each word stands by itself no matter at what pace one speaks. Actors extend this exercise even further by marking up their scripts. If a word is underlined, it means saying beat to himself after the word; if the word is circled, he takes two beats—beat, beat—and sometimes even three beats—beat, beat, beat. A dash going up means that the voice goes up; a dash at the end of the word going down means the voice is dropped.

Public personalities usually have very distinctive speech patterns; listen to Robert Morley, Orson Welles, Katharine Hepburn, Humphrey Bogart, Edward G. Robinson, Peter Lorre, Sandy Dennis, Boris Karloff, Spencer Tracy, Alfred Hitchcock and John Kennedy. Although their voices are unmistakably their own, they all have one thing in common, namely, that each , word , stands , by , itself. That is the professional's secret, and it explains why actors and announcers sound so different from the many people who telephone the hosts of radio talk shows.

Speaking may also be compared to playing a musical instrument. In addition to rhythm, one is required to play some passages loud and others soft. Too many people make the mistake of speaking in a monotone—no modulation of pitch—and frequently those with very strong voices fail to lower the voice in close quarters. The inaudible comma exercise will result in a completely natural sound, not in any way more affected than the speech of television announcers, with the possible exception of Howard Cosell.

In addition to giving your speech presence, it is desirable to add an agreeable personality, even when, one might say *especially* when, the subject itself is serious and not particularly agreeable.

There is a simple technique for achieving this, one I learned from a longtime friend, Dorothy Sarnoff. Since her retirement as an opera singer, Dorothy has become very successful teaching public speaking to executives, and boasts a distinguished clientele. Dorothy says, "Whenever you talk to anyone, make a conscious effort to create apples with your cheeks." Just think about it for a second. Making apples with your cheeks results in a kind of crinkling up of the eyes (laughing eyes). Try making apples with your cheeks in front of a mirror. You get an immediate twinkle in your eyes, a most agreeable expression on your face. Most newscasters do not follow this advice, but those few who do so look so much better. A bitter pill is easier to swallow with a little honey. In the same way, if you are communicating a serious message, it is received better if you don't *look* too serious.

Presence and personality are attributes of speech that can be developed through practice. Other improvements can be achieved just by recognizing the need to change certain things. Here are some examples.

1. Avoid Grammatical Mistakes

I blush to admit it, but until the age of twenty-seven I used irregardless for regardless, not realizing that it was a nonword, a word that to an educated listener would indicate lack of education, a wrong-side-of-the-tracks upbringing. And, just as bad, like Archie Bunker, I too bunked into a friend instead of bumped into a friend. Is it possible that you too misuse some of these other frequently confused words:

lay/lie	accept/except
sit/set	affect/effect
raise/rise	allude/elude
then/than	among/between
who/whom	leave/let

You might check a dictionary. Better yet, read *The Elements of Style* by William Strunk, Jr. and E. B. White, a short book that can be immensely helpful in clarifying the laws of grammar and word usage, making it much easier to speak out with confidence.

2. Don't Be Pedantic

In everyday speech, never use a three-syllable word if you can use a two-syllable word, and don't use a two-syllable word if you can use a one-syllable word. On the other hand, when writing an article or a speech, it is desirable to drop in one, maybe even two four-syllable words to indicate that you do have an extensive vocabulary. It might also be desirable to add a few esoteric quotes, easily found in *Bartlett's Familiar Quotations*.

3. Be Sincere

Conversation depends on mutual trust—something you can hear in the tone of voice as well as in the content of the actual remarks.

We have one friend, who with his wife does a great deal of entertaining. They are the most generous of hosts.

He in particular is always "on." That is, he welcomes you with an almost intense warmth and is actually oversolicitous of your comfort. The problem is that he tries so hard it makes one slightly uncomfortable.

We have another friend for whom everything is fabulous, which means that her compliments lose credibility because there is no gradation. It is the opposite of speaking in a monotone. Compliments should range from good to fabulous if they are to be meaningful. Sometimes, when a compliment is expected but not deserved and you don't want to sound insincere, try the standard response given to performers, "a very interesting interpretation," or to composers of avant-garde music, "a most interesting piece!"

Look at the person you are talking to, but do not carry it to an extreme or the opposite impression may result. One of my Custom Shop vice-presidents has a way of staring people into the ground when he talks to them. The staring is unrelieved. It makes one uncomfortable. It also makes him appear to be untrustworthy, as though he were overcompensating for some insincerity.

4. Don't Raise Your Voice

To raise the voice when one is angry becomes a dead giveaway about background. People with taste seldom scream or shout (and there is never a winner in any heated argument about politics). Therefore, present your point of view as eloquently as you can, but always with a friendly voice and face.

Similarly, in dealing with incompetence at the office, speak in a manner which does not diminish your own stature or suggest you are wanting in either sophistication or vocabulary. Instead of a loudly belligerent "I asked you to do this twice and it still hasn't been done" or "If you can't get it done and get it done quickly, I'm going to throw you out on your head!," try this: "Like every firm, we need good people and I expect you are doing your best; however, in this instance and in several other instances, your best hasn't been good enough. Unless you can do better than you have been doing, I'm afraid we'll have to part company."

5. Be Careful about Throat-Clearing

I do not have a strong voice, and never knew how to project it. Cocktail parties and large parties of any kind are particularly trying because the effort to make myself heard over the din exhausts me. At one point I decided there was something wrong with my throat, so I went to a specialist. He said there was nothing wrong with me except a lack of technique. So, he sent me to a speech therapist, Esti Freud, daughter-in-law of Sigmund Freud.

Esti listened to my tale of woe, then asked me to take off my jacket, lie down on the couch, unbuckle my belt, open the waistband of my trousers, and pull down my zipper. At the time, Esti was eighty so I couldn't imagine what was coming next. It was only the beginning of proper breathing exercises. As we advanced (I was permitted to zip up my pants and put on my jacket), she pointed out that I had a habit of clearing my throat. "Don't clear your throat, swallow it," she told me, explaining that this was much less wearing on the vocal cords. Since that time I have had five women in my employ who cleared their throats almost continuously. Three of the five were beautifully spoken: one a Ph.D., one an art major with a master's degree, and the third with a B.A. who was a lead singer in her church choir. I cured all five with the instructions contained in that one sentence: "Don't clear your throat, swallow it."

6. Don't Giggle

If you have a tendency to laugh when there really is nothing to laugh about, curb the habit. It is a nervous reaction that detracts from your dignity, is unattractive, and certainly unnecessary.

7. Be Aware of Your Hand Gestures

Some people use their hands excessively during conversation; others don't use them at all. In this as in most matters, a happy medium is best. Observe any good conversationalist and adopt those gestures with which you feel comfortable.

Try to keep your hands out of your pockets. Certainly, it is mildly offensive for a lawyer, accountant, or sales clerk to present his views with his hands in his pockets either in an office setting or on the lecture platform. If you need to hold onto something, look for the back of a chair or the lectern. One more thing about hands: Some people have a tendency to put their hands on people. People find this offensive. If you are one of those offenders, be sensitive to the vibrations that result from the laying on of hands.

Our trainees frequently had their hands in their pockets when they approached customers. Until it was pointed out to them, they were not even aware that they were doing it.

A Touch of Class on the Telephone

It is surprising to find that personalities change when people speak on the phone. Some people become aggressive; others, shy; and still others react to and assume the personality of the person to whom they are talking. Something about the anonymity of the telephone causes us to alter our personalities. There is, too, another aspect to this peculiar phenomenon. When we see a person, his appearance influences our ears. An attractive person projects a more pleasing sound than an unattractive person. We are not conscious of this, but the part does influence the whole; our reaction to one facet affects our reaction to the balance.

On the telephone, therefore, where your voice is the sole indication of the invisible you, you should *consciously* make an effort to speak in as warm and pleasant a voice as you can. How you sound is affected by your inner attitude as well as your facial expressions. A frown or a smile will literally show in your voice. It's virtually impossible to say you hate someone while smiling or that you love someone while inwardly seething, because physiological processes occur that correspond to your emotional attitude. For this reason, whenever my daughter Elizabeth answered the phone, I usually knew whether it was an attractive boy, an unattractive boy, a friend, a stranger, or a wrong number.

The power of the telephone to influence the voice is most dramatically demonstrated on an answering machine, where nearly everyone adopts the machine's impersonality and ends up sounding like a robot.

Almost without exception these machine-answering instructions are stuffy, redundant, or both. For example: "This is 555-4366. We are not at home to receive your call, but if you will leave your name, telephone number, the time and date of your call, and a brief message, we will return your call as quickly as we can. Remember, wait for the beep. 'Beep.'" More or less standard, but no humor and, even worse, redundant. Here's a suggestion for a short message you may want to try:

This is 555-4366. Sorry about the machine,
but it saves you the bother of calling later.
If you want to leave a message, wait for the beep.
And don't be nervous; you're not on the air.

or

Jean Kerr quotes this message left by some friends on their machine.

We shall not sleep,
We shall not slumber,
Unless you leave
Your name and number.

While I am at it, another minor irritant is "Have a nice day." I was told about a man who telephoned to make the necessary arrangements for his wife's interment, at the end of which the funeral director said, "Don't worry, we will take care of everything. Have a nice day." And that reminds me of a story Myron Cohen used to tell in a

Yiddish dialect. Myron called a funeral director and said, "My wife died, please to make the necessary arrangements for the funeral." The undertaker said, "But, Mr. Cohen, we buried your wife two years ago." Myron said, "Yes, but I remarried." And the undertaker replied, "Oh, really? Congratulations!"

3

How You Look

A man should look as good as he is—even better if possible.

> "You never get a second chance to make
> a first impression."
> —*Will Rogers*

IT MAY OCCUR to the reader that I give too much space to appearance, appearance being only an appurtenance of class. On the other hand, substance without the appurtenances diminishes one's class-scale rating. Therefore, the appurtenances deserve to have their proper space. Unfortunately, because the subject of appearance has never been part of the college curriculum, most people do not look as good as they might. If improvement in image is one of the reasons for reading this book, the space I give it is well deserved.

You will not improve your image unless you work at it. You must apply yourself just as an MBA studies to get a degree or a tennis player practices to become a champion.

My interest in clothes began seventy-two years ago. It was my father's unhappy duty to walk me to my first day at school. I was five; it was kindergarten. I would have none of it; I kicked my father and the school principal. I was dragged back into the street still screaming. The next day my mother tried her luck. By then I realized there was no choice, and calmed down. Mother's final instructions were, "Mortimer, sit next to a cleanly dressed girl." I took a seat between two cleanly dressed girls, Ruth Clayton and Ruth Bornman, both doctors' daughters, and I guess I have been sitting next to cleanly dressed women ever since.

In this chapter we will consider only the image projected by the clothes you wear and the effect it may have on your class scale rating. I devote a whole chapter to the subject because it is the one area in which competence seems to be almost completely lacking. Even though my cultural horizon was limited, I did have an early aptitude for clothes. When I was eighteen and should have known better, I wore spats and carried a cane. I discarded the spats, but still carry a cane.

If you were lucky enough to have been born with brains, personality, and the motivation to become an overachiever, you should have brains enough to project an image that reflects your competence. Actors are always dressed by highly paid professionals to project an image suited to the character being played. In like manner, you too should dress for the role you now play or hope to play. For those who are just beginning a career, think about this. If you do not have the appearance of a potential executive, it may never occur to anyone that you really are one.

Because most men lack guidance in buying and co-ordinating a wardrobe, the outer man seldom reflects inner brain power. Is creating a wardrobe complicated? Yes, if there are no guidelines. So, here are four simple rules that will color-coordinate your clothes—for the office, for weekends and for all social occasions—without impinging on your personal taste. Do *not* dismiss these four rules before you try them. Try them *precisely* as outlined and you will always look as good as you are.

Rule One: Wear two plains and a fancy (two solid colors but only one pattern)

A workday civilian uniform consists of three pieces: suit, shirt, and tie. Only one of the three should have a pattern, because two patterns fight each other. In other words, one pattern will not complement a second pattern, whereas a plain will. The plain looks better, the pattern looks better, and you look better.

Furthermore, a sophisticated use of solid colors is more flattering than the unsophisticated custom of mixing patterns. You may receive no compliments on the suit, shirt or tie, but you will receive many compliments on how well you look. "Have you been on vacation?" "You look marvelous." "Have you lost weight?" "You look as if you finally came into your inheritance," etc.

You buy a chalk stripe (pin stripe) suit because you like the pattern. Don't kill the pattern by forcing it to compete with patterns in your shirt or necktie. Two patterns cancel each other out, like ice cream and pickles. Ice cream tastes good, pickles taste good; but mix them, and they taste pretty bad. If your suit is black with a white chalk stripe, wear a plain gray or white shirt and a plain silver necktie, or a plain light blue shirt and plain light blue necktie.

A second example: If the suit is brown with a light blue glen plaid, the shirt should be plain blue and the tie plain light blue or tan.

Another example: If the suit is gray flannel, the shirt could be plain blue and the tie a gray-and-blue silk foulard print. The depth of the colors is an important consideration and is fully explained in Rule Three, which (logically) we will go to after Rule Two. The principle applies equally to gray and red, navy and white, tan and red, gray and yellow, etc.

Two plains and one fancy not only look better, they are also low key—a first step toward projecting an executive image. American men, unlike their European counterparts, frequently wear three patterns. If you think one pattern isn't fancy enough, remember that men look their very best in uniforms and in formal clothes, no patterns at all—plain black suit, plain white shirt, plain black tie.

Rule Two: Wear a base color with an accent color

The suit is *always* the base color. The shirt and/or tie provide the accent color. For example, you might wear a navy suit, pale yellow shirt, and yellow-and-navy tie. The base color is navy, the accent color is yellow, and the tie combines both colors—navy and yellow. Or the suit is gray, the shirt blue, and the tie gray and blue; base color gray, accent color blue. Or the suit could be brown, the shirt cream, and the tie cream and maroon, cream being a lighter shade of brown; base color brown, accent color maroon.

If you follow the first two rules consistently, you will be surprised at how easy it is to color-coordinate your entire wardrobe at the office and away from the office, on weekends, in the country, or on holiday. Shopping becomes easier too because you don't buy anything that doesn't color-coordinate with your existing wardrobe.

Rule Three: Balance dark with light and light with dark

If the suit is dark, shirt and tie should be light. If the suit is light, shirt and tie may be darker. If the suit is medium, shirt and tie may be medium to light. Thus, the overall effect will always be well balanced. The most common mistake is wearing dark and dark, coloring that is never complimentary to one's skin tone. For example, a navy suit (dark), blue end-on-end broadcloth shirt (darker than a plain blue), and a navy or maroon tie (dark) is not flattering. Try a navy suit, cream shirt and cream tie with a navy-and-light-blue pattern or stripe. Another example: Oxford gray suit (dark) with wine end-on-end broadcloth shirt (dark), and a wine-colored tie (dark)—*not* flattering. Try a white shirt and a light gray tie with a red-and-white pattern. Use the combinations suggested in the following chart, and the improvement in image will become immediately apparent.

Suit Color	Shirt Color	Tie Color	
		GROUND COLOR	PATTERN COLOR
Black	Pale gray broadcloth	Silver	Black and yellow
Dark	White broadcloth	White	Black and red
	Light blue broadcloth	Blue	Black and white
	Cream broadcloth	Cream	Black and yellow
	Yellow broadcloth	Yellow	Black and white
	White with gray stripe	Silver or yellow solid	
	White with gray check	Silver or yellow solid	
Navy	White broadcloth	White	Navy and light blue
Dark	Light blue broadcloth	Light blue	Navy and yellow
	Cream broadcloth	Cream	Navy and yellow
	Yellow broadcloth	Yellow	Navy and light blue
	White with blue stripe	Light blue or yellow solid	
	White with blue check	Light blue or yellow solid	
Brown	White broadcloth	White	Brown or tan
Dark	Light blue broadcloth	Blue	Brown or tan
	Cream broadcloth	Cream	Brown or tan
	Yellow broadcloth	Yellow	Brown or tan

Suit	Shirt	Tie	Accessory
	White with brown stripe	Tan solid	
	White with brown check	Tan solid	
Gray Flannel Medium	Blue end-on-end	Black	Blue
	Gray end-on-end	Gray	White or red
	Pink end-on-end	Black	Red
	Yellow broadcloth	Black	Yellow
	Red Bengal stripe	Black or red solid	
	Black/red tattersall check	Black or red solid	
Light Blue Tropical Light	White broadcloth	Navy	White and blue
	Cream broadcloth	Navy	Cream and blue
	Blue end-on-end	Navy	Light blue and yellow
	Pink end-on-end	Navy	Pink and blue
	Blue Bengal stripe	Blue or yellow solid	
	Navy/blue tattersall check	Blue or yellow solid	
Tan Tropical Medium	Cream broadcloth	Brown	Tan and cream
	Tan end-on-end	Brown	Tan and yellow
	Blue end-on-end	Brown	Blue and tan
	White with tan stripe	Brown solid	
	White with tan check	Brown solid	

Rule Four: Fit your shirt collar to the fourth dimension

The one article of clothing that will change your appearance more radically than anything else you own is a shirt collar that has been fitted to four dimensions instead of the usual two. The two dimensions usually are collar size (15, 15½, 16, etc.) and collar style. Contrast those simplistic concepts with the following four dimensions.

1. COLLAR BACK HEIGHT. The length of your neck determines precisely how high your collar should be in the *back*. Shirtmakers cut all collar styles in *five* different back heights. Depending on the length of your neck, collar back height will range from 1⅜ inches to 2¼ inches. If the shirt collar is cut to the proper back height, a man with a long neck (or short neck) will appear to have a normal neck. The longer the neck, the higher the collar should be in back. No friend will remark on the back height of your shirt collar; he or she will see only that you look better.

2. COLLAR FRONT HEIGHT. Whereas collar back height depends on the length of your neck, the front height depends on your age and the angle at which the neck sits on the body. When a man has turned forty and his neck begins to wrinkle, the collar band should be cut higher in front to cover those wrinkles. Wrinkles are not only an age give-away; they also create an over-the-hill image.

A pin collar is the best way to treat the wrinkled neck problem, and the one we recommend. The collar is made with eyelets, and a gold safety pin keeps the knot in place. It creates a military—shall we say, a more vigorous—look.

A man with a military bearing walks with his chin up

and head high. Other men carry their heads down. All this affects the front height and is taken into consideration when collars are individually designed.

3. COLLAR SIZE. Several years ago we selected a thousand first-order customers at random and checked their ready-made size (that is, the size they had been buying) against the collar size we made for them. There was an average *increase* in collar size of *three-quarters of an inch*. The variation ranged from a quarter-inch to an inch and a half—an increase, for example, from size 15 to size 16½. The occasional customer whose ready-made size was correct invariably had lost weight because of diet or illness. Every other man needs a shirt collar fitted to the quarter-inch, 15¼ or 15¾, not to the half-inch, 15½. Tight collars make men look fatter. In addition, tight collars wrinkle around the tie and expose a gap above the necktie because the tie slides down exposing the collar band.

This brings to mind the story about a man who gave up smoking to avoid lung cancer. He felt very much better, except for the fact that he put on eighteen pounds, suffered from severe headaches, and saw spots before his eyes. He went to his doctor, who, unhappily, told him he had an inoperable brain condition. The man was terribly upset, but being of a philosophical nature, decided to retire and do some of the things he had always wanted to do, one of them being, strangely enough, having his shirts custom-made. He told the shirtmaker he wore a 15½ inch collar and a 33 sleeve. The shirtmaker looked at him and said, "Mr. Jackson, are you kidding? Don't you know if you wear a collar that tight, you'll have terrible headaches, and, worse, you'll probably be seeing spots before your eyes."

TWO REASONS WHY MEN WEAR TIGHT COLLARS
1. Men gain weight.
2. Shirts shrink.

A man gains weight as he grows older because his body burns more calories at age twenty than it does at age forty. Therefore, unless he eats less each year, he gains weight. Because he tries suits on, he moves easily from 40 to 41, then 42, etc. But he never tries shirts on, so he continues to buy the same size until he is figuratively strangled. That is the first reason men wear tight collars, and it is a commonplace to see men at work unbuttoning collars and loosening neckties.

Every shirt shrinks. Shirting fabrics are Sanforized, but they all shrink about 2½ percent. Therefore, every shirt manufacturer of ready-mades makes an allowance for shrinkage—⅜ inch in the collar and ⅝ inch in the sleeves. So, a 15½ inch collar measures almost 16 inches when it is bought and shrinks to 15½ inches, the size originally bought.

If a collar is too tight, that's bad, but if it's too loose, that's equally bad. It makes a man look sickly or as if he had suffered a sudden weight loss as a result of illness.

4. COLLAR STYLE. There are only four basic collar styles: regular, button-down, pin and English spread. This might be a good time to clear up a common misunderstanding about collar styling. For example, a customer will say, "I like the collar that Cary Grant wears. Can you make it?" The answer, of course, is yes, because we are custom

shirtmakers. But what looks good on Cary Grant might not look good on the customer unless the back height, front height, and collar points are *modified* to complement the size and shape of his particular face. Only then would it be possible for the customer to wear a collar style that will look as good on him as it does on Cary Grant.

The key to a class image rests squarely on the collar because the collar frames the face. One must take into account collar height, size, and style, as well as the relationship between those factors and the individual neck and face. Unfortunately, no matter how skilled the shirtmaker, the collar will not look its best unless it is professionally laundered, preferably with a very light starch. Wash-and-wear shirts will pucker, not because of the fabric itself, but because of the stitching. No observer will say to himself, "Oh, the collar and cuffs are puckering," but they *will* observe that the wearer looks tacky. A class image means putting it all together—a properly fitted collar, a properly tied tie, and a suit, shirt and tie that have been properly color-coordinated. You can put it all together by thinking of your suit as a frame for shirts and ties that create a series of ever-changing pictures.

An Appurtenance of Class: Wearing Clothes Appropriate to the Occasion

If you wear your Sunday best to the office, what do you wear to a wedding, a dinner party, or a theater benefit? On the other hand, if you wear a turtleneck to the office on Friday, what are you going to wear to the football game on Saturday? People who rate high on the class scale generally know enough to wear clothes that are appropriate to the occasion in the same way, really, that the military does—by supplying battle dress, parade dress, and fatigue dress. Basically, a man has three occasions for which he should have appropriate clothes, regardless of his profession:

1. At the office
2. Dress-up for social occasions
3. Weekends in town or country

For weekday occasions, wear tweed or flannel suits (solid color only) with classic striped shirts and solid color ties (knit, rep, or grenadine). Alternate: solid color shirts in broadcloth, oxford or end-to-end broadcloth in pale colors (wear white only at night) complemented by color-coordinated patterned neckties in stripes or small patterned woven or printed foulard. The substitution of color for white creates a variety of flattering images that is also more appropriate for daytime wear. Save your dress-up suits—pin stripes, blacks and navies—for dress-up occasions. If, to provide yourself with variety, you want to wear a dress-up suit to the office, dress it down with a pale-colored shirt in blue, gray or yellow and a tie with a light colored background and pale blue, yellow or cream.

The importance of a plain tweed suit in a man's wardrobe is generally underestimated. A plain, tightly woven tweed suit, along with a gray flannel suit, should be the backbone of a daytime wardrobe. Strongly patterned tweed sport jackets and loosely woven or coarse tweed suits should be reserved for weekends.

For dress-up social occasions, the white shirt adds a

desirable festive touch to your dark suit, but reserve your white shirts for dress-up. That means after five. Pin striped suits worn with white collars on colored shirts are currently popular for dressy occasions.

If you project a class image during the week, you should project it on weekends as well. If you are no longer in high school, throw away those awful T-shirts with advertising on them and give away your jeans. Jeans are better suited to cowboys, plumbers and flower children. Jeans wrinkle badly, have no finish at the bottom, hang without flair, and are unflattering to any man with a waist measurement over 30. The myth that jeans are comfortable to wear is just that—a myth. Fashionably cut jeans are binding in all the wrong places. Standing may be okay, but when one sits down—well, who needs it? Replace your jeans with tan chinos. Chinos are crease-resistant and hang better because they have a finished bottom. Chinos can be dropped into the washing machine and need little or no ironing.

Add gray flannel slacks and a pair of white slacks, and you have a complete classic slack wardrobe that will take you through the entire year.

As for jackets, you need a minimum of one navy blazer (I recommend double breasted) and one patterned tweed jacket. There is a difference between a blazer and a sport jacket. The blazer, like the full-dress uniform of a naval officer, has gold buttons. The sport jacket, in contrast, has bone buttons. Some are very loosely woven and quickly wear out at the elbow. Because one English country gentle-man hated to part with a favorite sport jacket and elected to preserve the jacket by placing suede patches on the elbows, a new fashion was born—a fashion that by now has worked its way through the classes to the masses, a best seller at Alexander's.

At cocktail parties or dinner parties you'll be expected to wear a blazer, shirt, and tie. If it is less formal, omit the tie. But do not spread the shirt collar outside the collar or lapels of your blazer: that's considered high fashion only in Moscow. If you want to be daring, open up the collar and three buttons of your shirt, but keep the collar points inside the blazer.

Most summer evenings are cool enough so that one can be comfortable in a flannel blazer. But for daytime a tropical-weight blazer is desirable. White, pink, yellow or tan linen blazers are comfortable and flattering.

Perhaps I should outline a few complete outfits that will cover every weekend occasion.

1. Navy blue double-breasted blazer, gray flannel slacks, black loafers, black socks, blue oxford shirt, and neckties striped or patterned (background of light blue and patterned in navy and white—see chart on pages 76–77 for other possible color combinations).

2. Gray flannel slacks, gray crew-neck, cable stitch, lamb's wool sweater, blue Oxford shirt, no necktie.

3. Gray flannel slacks with Izod-type half-sleeve pullover in gray or light blue. Unless you have a 32-inch waist, wear the pullover outside, but sew a 3-inch hem on the bottom to provide a finished look similar to that of a pullover sweater. The popular Lacoste shirt—the half-sleeve shirt with the alligator on the chest—has become almost a uniform. It comes in twenty different shades, requires

little or no ironing, and because it is knitted, resists wrinkling.

4. If you are a swinging single or even part of a swinging couple, dazzle friends with black or purple velveteen slacks. Forget corduroy. It's too stiff and drapes badly. Velveteen is soft to the touch and hangs well.

5. Tan chinos with a tan half-sleeve Izod shirt for summer wear and a tan turtleneck for cooler weather with turtleneck worn outside your slacks. This look can be varied with a patterned tweed jacket. Wear a tan jacket with tan chinos and gray tweed jacket with gray flannel slacks. The tan chinos may be augmented with tan gabardine slacks which are rich-looking but not for working around the house. For golf the chinos and a tan Izod shirt are worn with brown golf shoes. Wear gray flannels and a black or gray turtleneck with black golf shoes on cooler days.

6. For tennis, wear white shorts and a white boat-neck T-shirt (if you can find one). If not, try a white crew neck. The no-collar shirt is recommended because perspiration quickly causes tennis collars to crumple. White is worn for tennis because it reflects the sun's rays. In contrast, color absorbs the sun's rays, making for undesirable heat and perspiration.

7. For summer lunch, wear white slacks with a white or yellow knitted cotton crew neck worn over a white or yellow Oxford shirt. Try a yellow belt, yellow espadrilles, no socks. You might carry a yellow dacron and linen blazer with white buttons and wear traditional sunglasses. As an

alternate try a pair of yellow linen slacks, worn with yellow espadrilles, no socks, and a yellow Izod-type shirt.

8. For cooler weather, add a poplin windbreaker with a stand-up collar that when closed is similar to, but not the same as, the collar that a priest wears. Usually quite becoming with a turtleneck.

The few outfits listed above will carry you through any holiday anywhere in any weather, and your own imagination permits you to add variations.

Another word about color coordination. The key to a class image on weekends rests not only on what you wear, but the concept of monochromatic and bichromatic.

Monochromatic color ensembles consist of only one color—different shades of browns and tans, or navy and blues or black, grays and white. Everything is included in a monochromatic scheme. Shoes, slacks, shirts, blazers, sport jackets, sweaters, jackets, hats, gloves, topcoats, car coats, windbreakers, raincoats—everything in a single color range.

A bichromatic color scheme is simply a monochromatic ensemble that includes a single accent color—base color gray, accent color blue, etc. But if clothes are a nuisance, forget the accent color. I know one thing for sure: you will be surprised at how much richer the clothes you now own look once you begin wearing them strictly by color.

A Touch of Class in Accessories

Let's finish the picture with a few pointers you may want to consider in the matter of accessories.

SHOES. In warm weather, many men wear tennis sneakers as a catchall, even though there are good-looking casual shoes that are more fun to wear. Get yourself a pair of white shoes and a pair of tan. There are also wonderful sandals and espadrilles from Spain. Each year produces a new series of inexpensive and attractive sport shoes.

For social occasions, you may want Gucci-type loafers, one pair in black and one pair in tan, with leather soles, plus shoes with thick rubber soles for walking in the rain. Laced-up hiking boots are practical and much-needed for hiking. They give necessary support for long walks and help to avoid sprained ankles when walking on rough terrain. They are usually made of unfinished cowhide to better camouflage dust from the road.

SOCKS. You will need solid-color socks in black, Oxford gray, and brown. In summer, wear tan, blue and white. And even if your wife knits them specially for you, avoid patterned socks.

Socks should fit over the calf. It's a real turn-off to see a patch of hairy skin visible between the tops of anklets and the bottoms of trousers. Over-the-calf socks are self-supporting.

Burlington Mills has come up with an innovation: socks that eliminate foot odor. They are identified by a green stripe knitted across the toes. They come in all cotton, all polyester, all wool, or any of the three blended with polyester. One size fits all, and they are reasonably priced. They are available in over-the-calf length, and they do stay up. Having tried the rest, I found them to be the best.

ATTACHÉ CASES. For business, carry an attaché case rather than a briefcase. Placed on your lap, the attaché case becomes a portable desk when you travel. And, obviously, for the very small additional expense, leather is preferable to vinyl. The difference does show.

WALLETS. I don't carry a wallet, because wallets are bulky; they stretch my suit out of shape and therefore put me out of shape. Anything that needs to be carried in a wallet can just as easily be carried in my attaché case or the glove compartment of my car. I carry bills in my right-hand trouser pocket, folded over my American Express card. Keys are in my left-hand pocket on a key chain. All other credit cards, my driver's license and pictures of my wife and children are in my attaché case, as are my reserve eyeglasses. In other words, there is no visible bulk anywhere in my clothing. My address book is also kept in my attaché case. An index card in my breast pocket is always available to jot down ideas, appointments, etc.

Men's shoulder bags and men's clutch purses do not present a desirable image.

HANDKERCHIEFS. I recommend using pure linen handkerchiefs. Linen is more absorbent, and the quality is immediately apparent. Have your handkerchiefs monogrammed. Why not? You wear out only five handkerchiefs a year, and a monogrammed linen handkerchief can be bought for about $7.50. A finishing touch that projects the right image. Do *not* reuse yesterday's messed-up handkerchief.

POCKET SQUARES. Silk foulard squares add an elegant touch for the man who carries his clothes with a certain air. Cary Grant and former New York City mayor John Lindsay are two good examples. I have tried pocket squares, but even though I carry clothes well, I have never been comfortable with a handkerchief in my breast pocket, and I don't wear one. If you like the look, however, I have three suggestions you may want to consider:

1. Use silk rather than white linen.

2. If you are wearing three plains, wear a pattern that contains the base color and the accent color of your ensemble.

3. If you are wearing two plains and a pattern, use a solid color silk pocket square that matches the accent color of your ensemble.

JEWELRY. There is not much that can be said about men's jewelry, except:

1. A wedding band on the left hand adds substance and keeps a married man free of undesirable entanglements.

2. A ring on the little finger—for example, a gold ring with black onyx—is decorative. However, a gold ring with a diamond looks better on a woman's hand. If you own one, this is the perfect time to sell it.

3. Cuff links and collar pins add a nice touch, as do identification bracelets. All should be gold if you can afford it, gold-filled if you cannot.

4. In the 1960s, flower children and hippies went to great pains to adorn themselves. Having little real cash to spend on clothes, they took their cues from the American Indian and turned to paint and beads. In the 1970s the beads turned to necklaces for men, with various symbols proclaiming their faith: the cross, the Star of David, the fertility symbol, etc. Body jewelry was displayed in Harry

Belafonte fashion: a sport shirt worn open to the navel. It's a nice look for hippies.

ROBES. There is nothing as abused as that comfortable old robe, which too many men wear until it literally falls apart. It is neither a compliment to one's wife or to oneself. Two suggestions:

1. Wear a floor-length robe. The robe I recommend is velour because the texture is as rich as velvet. Because velour is a knit and generally made of some form of nylon, it is practically indestructible. Throw it into the washing machine; it comes out clean-smelling with no trace of a wrinkle. Velour robes are generally designed so that one size fits all, with large loose-hanging three-quarter sleeves. Light blue, silver gray or white are generally more flattering than black, brown or navy.

2. In the summertime you might switch to a floor-length white terry-cloth robe, that can double as an after-swim wrap. Or you may want to consider a floor-length Japanese kimono-type cotton robe.

MAKEUP. Do you look better with a suntan? Most men do. Unfortunately, the sun is the most common cause of skin cancer. Exposure to the sun also leads to premature aging and wrinkles, and gives your skin a leathery look.

A fresh suntan is always becoming but after two weeks, the tan turns a yellowish brown, a color that is not becoming. On the other hand, city pallor, a look familiar to most urban dwellers, is not becoming either. All women know this and use makeup to compensate.

Happily, there is a product for men that offers the advantages of a fresh suntan with none of the disadvantages: the bronzing gel marketed by Estée Lauder's Clinique. Aside from making you look better, it is also a skin moisturizer. Properly applied, bronzing gels *never* look artificial, because the gel is totally invisible.

My best advice, however, is moderation. Use the bronzer *lightly* on the forehead, nose, and cheekbones *only*. Don't try for a look that says you've just returned from two weeks in Palm Beach. Rather, make it look as though you had taken a long walk on a sunny day in May. The result would be a slight tan on your forehead, nose, and cheekbones.

Finally, take a tip from your barber, who applies talcum with a towel after shaving you. Apply face powder with a powder puff, but don't use too much. Bronzing gel and face powder, properly applied, never look artificial.

SCENTS. Scents make sense for men only when used sparingly. When a woman kisses you hello, she will be aware of it. But if she becomes aware of it when she is two feet away, you have lowered your class scale rating. No one should smell you coming.

The Timeless Look for Women of Class

It is interesting that I can be in a room with a hundred people, yet if a woman walks in who wears clothes well, I see it immediately. The image is unmistakable and is, without question, one of the desirable appurtenances of class. So, you may wonder what it is that makes it so immediately apparent. The answer is simple. The woman who projects such an image has created a complete picture, a picture that is *not* based exclusively on a new Galanos dress or the latest

Calvin Klein. It is only when the picture is complete, from top to bottom, that one makes a statement, and such statements are usually timeless.

Unlike men, women have been conditioned to do everything they can to make themselves look attractive. Unfortunately, the fashion industry (designers, fashion magazines and the fashion press) relies on radical change (a synonym for fashion) to increase sales. These year-in, year-out changes serve only to create confusion and, worse, unnecessary spending because clothes are thrown away long before they are worn out. The suggestions that follow create a timeless look that rates high on our class scale, and completely bypasses fashion. There are five simple concepts to consider:

1. The Picture Frame Concept
2. The Color Coordination Concept
3. The Accessory Concept
4. A Fit-and-Fashion Concept
5. The Plan (putting it all together)

The principles are not much different from those suggested for men. The concept of base color and accent color is a concept already understood by most women, as is the concept of not mixing patterns. You will never find a woman wearing a polka-dot dress with a striped handbag and a paisley scarf. Women know better because they have been programmed to care for their appearance.

The Picture Frame Concept

Eye contact usually takes place above the waist, at restaurants, at one's desk, at board meetings, etc.; therefore, you get better value when you buy expensive detailing that makes you look better above the waist as opposed to expensive detailing below the waist. So, we will concentrate on creating pictures that dress up or flatter the face and bosom.

The picture frame is created by the skirt, vest, jumper, or suit. Pictures are created with blouses, scarves, bows, belts and jewelry. Intelligently color-coordinated, they create a never-ending series of different looks.

We are going to create forty different pictures so you can look different five days a week for eight weeks without repeating a single costume. Not bad, right? I suggest that you buy nothing until you have prepared a complete plan. It's easy and it's fun.

The Color Concept

Base colors, usable nine to ten months a year are black, navy, brown, gray and burgundy. Base colors for summer wear are white, tan, yellow, light blue and, in fact, any pastel shade that complements your coloring. In planning your costumes, you should select your colors carefully. Unless your clothing budget is unlimited, it is advantageous to exploit one color—let's say, black—completely before moving on to another base color—let's say, brown.

Hair color and eye color must be considered before establishing a basic color sequence. If you're a blonde, most colors are becoming. If you have blue eyes and brown hair, start with navy instead of black. If you have blue eyes and black hair or gray hair, black should be your starting color. Every base color requires matching shoes, handbag and gloves. Generally speaking, black is worn in fall and winter, and navy is worn in the spring. Burgundy, taupe and gray are frequently worn as alternates to black. It is smart not to jump around. After you have pushed one color as far as you can, move on to a second color. Black and navy are dressy if worn with satin. Brown and burgundy are usually worn for less formal occasions.

The Accessory Concept

Unfortunately, most women are not fully appreciative of the improvement in image that can result from a well-planned use of jewelry. It is a common mistake to wear one or two favorite, and perhaps valuable, pieces of jewelry that, although beautiful in themselves, do not necessarily relate to every costume. I would add to those valuable pieces lots and lots of color-coordinated costume jewelry. In addition, I would add lots of scarves, bows, removable collars, vests, jumpers, blouses, etc., all the inexpensive ways to change the look of a basic outfit.

What about my engagement ring? Shouldn't I wear that every day? Well, there is no law against wearing it every day, but to your friends and family it quickly becomes invisible. So, I suggest that it be worn for dress-up occasions when, hopefully, it can take its place with one or

two other pieces of jewelry that may also include diamonds
—diamond earrings, pin or necklace.

Change your accessories frequently, that is, with each
change of costume. "An accessory," says Webster, "is an
object not essential in itself, but adding to the beauty or
effectiveness of something else." When it comes to accessories, quantity is more important than quality, and color
is most important of all. If you can afford both quantity
and quality, so much the better. But wearing the same necklace and earrings day in and day out is boring. A wide
variety of colors in necklaces, earrings, bracelets, pins, and
scarves will give your costumes a continually different
look.

If you decide to wear solid gold earrings with a particular outfit, wear only gold—necklace, bracelet, ring and
pin. Don't mix gold with pearls or with precious or semi-
precious stones unless it is used as a setting. You really
should have a complete line of costume jewelry—rubies,
sapphires, emeralds, amethysts, malachite, tigereye, ivory,
coral, pearls and onyx. If you can't afford the real thing,
substitute gold plate, glass or plastic. If your rubies are real
and your pin 14-karat, only you, your family, and your
closest friend will know the difference. The image created
by red glass or gold plate will be the same.

Buy an inexpensive watch. Buy a quartz movement. It
will keep perfect time, and you can find an enormous
variety at $30 to $40. Look for a style that permits you to
substitute different watchbands so you can color-coordinate
them with the rest of your costume. If you have an expensive gold watch, save it for those times when you are
wearing gold.

A belt is an important accessory, and should be given full attention. Never wear a self-belt—it cheapens your dress. The width of your belt depends more on figure and less on fashion. A belt is needed to define a waistline and add a finishing touch. Generally, belts pick up the base color. A leather belt is the main step in converting a skirt and blouse into a costume.

Your ultimate goal is to look well-groomed and understated. You accomplish this by rotating the various components of your wardrobe to continually work out new combinations.

The Concept of Fit and Fashion

Don't Buy Size, Buy Fit. If you are fat, your clothes should be easy fitting to make you look less fat. If you are skinny, your clothes should be easy fitting to make you look less skinny. Clothes that fit on the easy side will always look more expensive than clothes fitted to the snug side. Most women buy clothes on the snug side, and the reason would be funny if it weren't so sad. Once a woman finds a size 10 dress that fits her properly, she establishes, in her own mind, that she is a 10; therefore, any dress marked 12 or 14 is considered to be too large, even though it fits better. While this might seem like an exaggeration, it is based on years of experience with women at the Custom Shop and really is the reason so many women wear clothes that are too tight. Our federal government has not regulated women's sizes the way they have regulated men's sizes; therefore, a 10 from one manufacturer measures the same as a 12 or even a 14 from another manufacturer. All three are really the same size. Henri Bendel even carries a size 2 (legitimately, a 6). So, ignore the size on the label and make sure the fit is on the easy side. There should never be a pull across the bosom.

Now, what about fashion? My advice is to ignore it unless the current fashion happens to be a perfect complement to your face and figure. Despite the fact that fashion changes are radical, classic clothes are always available. They have become classics because they are always in good taste and always in style.

Therefore: DON'T BUY SIZE, BUY FIT AND IGNORE FASHION UNLESS IT FITS YOUR NEEDS.

How do you determine what your line is; that is, what look is best for your figure? You will find it by accident. You try on a model (or models) that does wonders for your particular figure. Once you have found it (or them), that is what you search for in all future shopping. If you can't find it, it may be easier and even less expensive to have the original copied by a local dressmaker, using different fabric, different color and different detailing. In Westport, Connecticut, a relatively affluent community, a local dressmaker will make an uncomplicated dress for you for seventy-five dollars, labor only. Fabrics are now forty-five inches wide (sometimes sixty inches wide), so a dress takes only two or two and one-half yards. And there is an endless array of fabrics available at $7 to $10 per yard. In contrast, there are very few quality dresses on the market for $100. If you are terribly lucky, you may have a figure that looks good in any style. If so, consider yourself blessed.

The Plan (Putting It All Together)

Chief executives know that they cannot run a business without a plan: planned inventory, planned budget expenditures, planned sales, etc. In the same way, it is not possible to make efficient use of your clothing budget without making a plan.

Try My Modular Concept

You will need three or four skirts, three or four vests, twelve to eighteen blouses, three or four belts plus lots and lots of costume jewelry. As you will see, with the modular concept (mixing components), you create dozens of different costumes without repeating yourself. And the modular concept saves you money, too.

Your picture frame (skirt, vest, suit or jumper) should be solid colors with no patterns at all. Save the patterns for blouses, scarves, ties or jewelry. If the picture frame is dark —navy, brown, black or Oxford gray—your picture— blouse, scarf—should be light. If your picture frame is light —white, yellow, red, tan, pink—your accessories can be dark (base color black, accent color white; base color white, accent color black, etc.).

A variety of costumes is more easily achieved by changing the area that frames the face, namely, the blouse. The concept of a modular wardrobe calls for a wide variety of blouses, and I suggest that your blouses be bought over a period of twelve to eighteen months, one each month.

I am recommending vests instead of or in addition to jackets. A well-tailored jacket costs about $200. A comparable vest costs $40. Besides, the vest makes a better showcase for your figure, your blouse and your accessories. If you prefer jackets to vests and are in a position to afford them, that is fine because the principles of color-coordination remain the same.

In addition to the vested look, I am including one black dress so you can see that the same principles apply. Our plan includes four base colors—three dark, black, navy and wine, and one light, taupe. Taupe can be combined with black, navy, wine and brown. However, we are not including brown in our forty costumes because you would have to buy brown shoes, handbag, belt and gloves. I will begin with five different looks for one black dress, but the principles apply to any other basic dress in all four base colors. However, I recommend more blouses than dresses because a blouse costs $30 to $40, whereas a dress costs $125 to $200. Yet a different blouse creates the same change of image as a different dress. The dress is the picture; the blouse is the picture. By concentrating on blouses, you extend the variety permitted by your budget. I'm going to suggest forty different costumes, a different look every working day for eight weeks, and I'll begin with a basic black dress with a jewel neckline, a neckline that lends itself to different treatments.

COSTUME NO. 1—Black dress, jewel neckline, black shoes, handbag, belt and gloves. Gold earrings, a gold necklace, gold bracelet and/or bangles and gold ring.

COSTUME NO. 2—Everything the same as Costume No. 1, but substitute pearl earrings, pearl necklace, pearl pin and a pearl bracelet for the gold.

COSTUME NO. 3—Instead of the pearl necklace, substitute a white chiffon scarf held in place with a pearl pin. Put a black band on your watch.

COSTUME NO. 4—Same black dress. This time the accent is wine. Wine shoes, hose, belt, handbag, gloves, wine strap on your watch. Ruby earrings, necklace, bracelet, pin and ring.

COSTUME NO. 5—Wear a detachable white piqué collar —there are various models (Peter Pan, Buster Brown, clown, etc.)—or white lace collar. Wear it with pearl earrings, necklace, bracelet. It would look just as good if your jewelry were all gold.

By now it is obvious that there are still other ways of accessorizing your basic black dress, and that would be equally true if the basic dress were navy, white, brown, gray or tan. Thus far I have suggested only the white chiffon scarf and the detachable collar, but the look can also be changed by using a Hermes-type printed silk scarf folded into a triangular shape and held together on the shoulder with a pin. A black dress can also be worn with emeralds (no green shoes) and diamonds if you have them. You may substitute rhinestones, but I do not recommend them. Nor would I recommend fake diamonds. Even though they are fairly expensive and look like the real thing, they would serve only to call attention to the fact that you couldn't afford a real diamond. This is not true when substituting red glass for rubies or blue glass for sapphires.

But let's be stingy and select only five looks for the black dress. Wear it weeks one, three, five, seven, and eight. In other words, you wear it only five times in two months; but each time you wear it, it will look completely different. Each time you wear it, you'll project the image of a woman whose appurtenances rate high on our class scale. Although black is popular in winter and navy in spring, there are all the other colors in between. Nevertheless, the first two base colors that you decide on should be those which you find most becoming.

If funds are limited, I recommend 100% polyester crepe, foulard and/or satin for your basic dresses and blouses. Polyester is wrinkle-resistant, inexpensive and has the precise draping qualities of pure silk. In addition, polyester is machine-washable and won't shrink out of shape. Wear cotton if you prefer and if you can afford the maintenance, but cotton wrinkles badly and is hard to iron.

In the spring, prints are popular, and you may want to buy one. Bear in mind, however, that the dress itself then becomes a picture because you cannot really change the look with accessories. The print *becomes* the picture. If you decide to buy a print, make it classic—a polka dot or classic stripe in a classic model, a line that will have a five-year fashion life.

Let's look at your other options. As I said, suits are expensive, running from $250 to $500. A suit too tends to become the picture (because it is the total look), and a very expensive picture at that. In contrast, a vest creates an image similar to a suit, but, because it is only part of a costume, it can be worn either as the base color, your picture frame or as an accent color, your picture. This permits a greater variety of pictures with fewer expenditures. Vests are not easy to find, but once you find a vest you like, it is easy to have a local dressmaker copy it in colors and fabrics that contrast or match your two or three favorite skirts.

The man-tailored suit is particularly good for the transitional seasons—spring and fall—when it can be worn without a coat. If you can afford it, two classic suits, one for spring and one for fall, deserve an honored place in your wardrobe.

The man-tailored jacket was designed to complement a man's figure by building up his shoulders and chest. But a man-tailored jacket does not flatter a female figure. I don't want to be misunderstood. If you have a boyish figure, tall and slender with small breasts, the man-tailored suit is very becoming. Some career women believe that the bosom looks better covered, and a man-tailored suit does that perfectly. However, there is no valid reason to conceal a feminine figure, and I recommend two alternatives to the man-tailored jacket: the vest and the dressmaker suit, the jacket of which has no padding and comes in a variety of styles.

Now, let us work with what you already own. To begin with, take everything you own out of closets and drawers—clothes, accessories, coats, shoes, bags, jewelry, everything! Next, separate everything by color—blouses, vests, sweaters, skirts, jumpers, jackets, suits and accessories. Draw up a chart similar to the one on page 104 so you can list your completed costumes by number.

Base colors are black, navy, wine and taupe and/or

brown; summer base colors are white, tan or any pastel shade that complements your coloring. Now, create as many pictures as you can with one base color, for example, black, before moving on to a second color. Some costumes will look okay while others will look smashing. Write down only the smashing combinations.

List your complete costumes by number. Set an initial goal of ten costumes per base color. If you go through this procedure once, you are set for six to nine months. Most costumes will run for years because you are dealing with a classic look. When you write up your plan, list every item needed to complete each costume.

A good retail merchant knows that he must clean out his inventory twice a year by weeding out the losers. The equivalent for you would be to throw away clothes that don't fit or really are worn out. Then, throw away your shopping mistakes. You won't know how limited your working inventory actually is unless you clean it out once a year.

A Sample of What Your Costume Chart May Look Like

Skirt/Jumper/ Suit/Dress	Blouse	Vest/Jacket/ Sweater	Jewelry	Accessories	I Need to Buy
Navy skirt	White satin blouse with third button open	Navy vest	Two long pearl necklaces, pearl earrings and bracelet	Natural hose, navy shoes, bag, belt, gloves	Pearl ring, navy pantyhose
Taupe skirt	Wine blouse with separate matching bow worn as ascot	Taupe vest	Amethyst earrings, ring and pin (holds ascot in place)	Wine hose, shoes, bag, gloves and belt	Amethyst ring, wine gloves
Taupe skirt	Taupe and black stripe mandarin-collar blouse		Gold necklace, ring, earrings and pin	Black hose, shoes, belt, bag and gloves	
Wine skirt	Pink blouse	Wine vest	Gold earrings, pin, bracelet, ring	Wine hose, shoes, bag, gloves and belt	Pink and wine scarf
Black dress			Long pearl necklace, pearl earrings, pearl bracelet, pearl ring	Black or taupe hose, black bag, black gloves and black belt	Pearl pin

Your "I Need to Buy" List

As you plan your costumes, you will find that you need to buy a certain accessory—a brooch or pin, a vest, whatever, to complete a costume. Therefore, your chart must have an "I Need to Buy" column. You shop only with a list of specific items in specific colors that are needed to complete or create new costumes.

I cannot urge you too strongly to make your chart. Every Sunday you can list the costumes you will want to wear during the coming week—No. 12 on Monday, No. 39 on Tuesday, No. 19 on Wednesday, and so on. Vary your base colors. Choose from your black one day, taupe the next and burgundy the day after that. A boost in morale results from always looking your best and always looking different.

Sheena Paterson, editor of the *Toronto Star*, puts it this way: "For me, there is nothing more intimidating than throwing open the closet in the morning and being met with a jumble of skirts, blouses, and dresses." She has solved her problem by keeping her recipes right on her closet door—and that is where your chart belongs.

Simple? That is exactly the point, and you will find it great fun besides. By putting your wardrobe in writing, a job that requires four hours, six at the most, you accomplish the following:

1. You see that an accessory can be worn with more than one base color and can be listed many times. For

example, a pink blouse can be worn with black, brown, navy or burgundy.

2. You never wake up asking yourself, "What shall I wear today?"

3. You are no longer tempted to make the common mistake of buying on impulse. Your "I Need to Buy" column will tell you exactly what you need, and you will buy only (and precisely) what you need.

4. You make use of everything you own, and you change your picture daily.

5. Things you never wore suddenly become very wearable because they are now properly color-coordinated and accessorized.

6. Finally, you spend less but look as though you spent more.

And, don't overlook the jumper. It is becoming to most figures. Add to that the fact that a jumper tends to project a nostalgic, schoolgirl image at any age. The jumper serves as an excellent picture frame for the picture—your blouse and accessories. Jumpers come in many different styles. Find the style that is most flattering for your particular figure.

To the forty costumes that have been outlined, you may add your dresses, suits, sweaters, and miscellaneous apparel. My costumes are basically designed for fall, winter and spring, although some will be wearable forty-five of the ninety days of summer. If you like my ideas, adopt the same principles for your summer costumes. Planning, color-coordinating and accessorizing—concepts that, upon reflection, are so simple one wonders why it needs to be written at all. But, look around, and you will see why it is needed.

Aside from the basic color combinations (navy, white, etc.), here's a list of other possibilities.

gray/wine   olive/wine
gray/yellow   olive/red
gray/scarlet   olive/purple

black/pink   green/red
black/tan   green/yellow
                   green/khaki

tan/yellow
tan/wine   light brown/medium blue
tan/olive   light brown/white

I am suggesting the following eighteen blouses that you should consider buying. The separate matching bow can be worn three ways: one, as an ascot; two, as a large cat-whisker bow; and three, with the collar open, tied in the familiar sailor's knot—the black scarf sailors wear with their middies. Any five of the blouses can be bought with pleated fronts and/or dickey bosoms. Although I list only polyester satin and polyester crepe, there are many other fabrics that would be just as suitable.

1. White crepe blouse, with separate matching bow
2. White satin, pointed-collar blouse (peek-a-boo)
3. White crepe jewel-neckline blouse

4. White satin mandarin-collar blouse
5. White crepe blouse with wing collar
6. White and navy polka-dot blouse
7. White and wine striped blouse
8. Wine blouse with separate matching bow/ascot
9. Wine satin-stripe blouse
10. Pink crepe blouse with separate matching large bow
11. Scarlet crepe blouse with pointed collar
12. Taupe ascot blouse with separate matching bow
13. Taupe and wine printed foulard blouse
14. Taupe and navy printed or woven plaid blouse
15. Taupe and black striped blouse
16. Light blue blouse with white round collar
17. Royal blue mandarin-collar blouse
18. Black mandarin-collar blouse

The pin is worn only on the vest or jacket. There are two possible positions: the usual top left and on the vest, the unusual lower left-hand corner. Most pins are too heavy to be worn on the blouse itself, except when the collar is worn closed. Then the pin is pinned directly over the button that closes the collar, in which case it replaces the bow tie as a finishing touch.

In the following, only the shoe color will be noted; for example, black shoes will *always* be worn with black handbag, black belt and black gloves or wine shoes with wine belt, handbag and gloves, etc.

COSTUME NO. 6—Navy skirt; white crepe blouse with pointed collar and separate matching large bow; navy vest; pearl earrings, ring, pin and bracelet; natural, white, or navy hose; navy shoes.

COSTUME NO. 7—Navy skirt; white satin blouse open to third button (peek-a-boo); two long pearl necklaces, pearl earrings, ring and bracelet; navy hose; navy shoes.

COSTUME NO. 8—Navy skirt; white crepe blouse with jewel neckline; gold choker, gold ring, gold earrings, gold bracelets; navy hose; navy shoes.

COSTUME NO. 9—Navy skirt; white wing-collar blouse; navy vest; printed white and navy foulard bow; sapphire (blue) earrings, bracelet, ring and pin; navy, natural or white hose; navy shoes.

COSTUME NO. 10—Navy skirt; scarlet crepe blouse with pointed collar; sapphire earrings, ring, necklace and bracelet; navy hose; navy shoes.

COSTUME NO. 11—Navy skirt; pink blouse with separate matching large bow, pointed collar; navy vest; coral earrings, ring, pin and bracelet; navy hose; navy shoes.

COSTUME NO. 12—Navy skirt; white and navy polka-dot blouse; navy vest; pearl necklace, ring, earrings and bracelet; white, navy or natural hose; white, navy or natural gloves (same as hose); navy shoes.

COSTUME NO. 13—Navy skirt; woven taupe and blue plaid blouse; sapphire necklace, ring, earrings and pin; navy or taupe hose; navy shoes.

COSTUME NO. 14—Navy skirt; light blue blouse with white round collar and separate solid blue bow tie; navy vest; sapphire earrings, ring, pin and bracelet (multi-bangles); navy hose; navy shoes.

COSTUME NO. 15—Taupe skirt; black and beige shirt-maker crepe blouse; onyx earrings, ring, necklace and bracelet; taupe hose; black shoes.

COSTUME NO. 16—Taupe skirt; wine satin-stripe blouse; ruby necklace, earrings and pin; taupe vest; wine hose; wine shoes.

COSTUME NO. 17—Taupe skirt; wine blouse with separate matching bow worn as ascot; taupe vest; ruby earrings, ring and pin (pin holds the ascot in place); wine hose; wine shoes.

COSTUME NO. 18—Taupe skirt; taupe ascot blouse; navy vest; sapphire earrings, pin and bracelet; taupe stockings; navy shoes.

COSTUME NO. 19—Taupe skirt; printed taupe and wine blouse; taupe vest; ruby necklace, earrings, ring, bracelet and pin; wine hose; wine shoes.

COSTUME NO. 20—Taupe skirt; navy and taupe plaid blouse with plain navy bow; sapphire earrings, ring, bracelet; navy hose; taupe shoes.

COSTUME NO. 21—Taupe skirt; royal blue mandarin-collar blouse; pearl necklace, ring, pin and earrings; taupe hose; taupe shoes.

COSTUME NO. 22—Taupe skirt; wine satin mandarin-collar blouse; ruby necklace, earrings, pin, ring and bracelet; wine hose; wine shoes.

COSTUME NO. 23—Taupe skirt; light blue blouse with round white collar, worn open; long sapphire necklace, sapphire earrings and ring; taupe hose; taupe shoes.

COSTUME NO. 24—Taupe skirt; black mandarin-collar blouse; taupe vest; onyx necklace, earrings, ring and pin; black hose; black shoes.

COSTUME NO. 25—Taupe skirt; taupe blouse with separate matching bow worn as ascot; black vest; onyx earrings, ring and bracelet; taupe hose; black shoes.

COSTUME NO. 26—Black skirt; white crepe blouse with pointed collar and separate matching bow; black vest; pearl earrings, ring and bracelet; natural or white hose; black shoes.

COSTUME NO. 27—Black skirt; white satin pointed-collar blouse worn open (peek-a-boo); two long pearl necklaces; pearl ring and earrings; black mesh hose; black shoes.

COSTUME NO. 28—Black skirt; white satin blouse with stand-up mandarin collar; onyx earrings, necklace, pin, ring and bracelet; black mesh hose; black shoes.

COSTUME NO. 29—Black skirt; white wing-collar blouse with black bow tie; black vest; pearl earrings, ring and bracelet; dark tan hose; black shoes.

COSTUME NO. 30—Black skirt; white crepe Pierrot-collar blouse; black vest; onyx choker, ring, earrings and bracelet; white or natural hose; black shoes.

COSTUME NO. 31—Black skirt; taupe and black stripe blouse with pointed collar worn open (peek-a-boo); gold choker, earrings, ring and bangles; dark tan hose; black shoes.

COSTUME NO. 32—Wine skirt; white satin pointed-collar blouse; long string of pearls, pearl earrings, pin, ring and bracelet; wine hose; wine shoes.

COSTUME NO. 33—Wine skirt; wine and white satin stripe blouse with tailored collar; ruby earrings, necklace, pin, ring and bracelet; wine hose; wine shoes.

COSTUME NO. 34—Wine skirt; white jewel-neckline blouse; ruby choker, bracelet, ring, earrings; white hose; wine shoes.

COSTUME NO. 35—Wine skirt; light blue blouse with round collar; long pearls, earrings and ring; wine hose; wine shoes.

COSTUME NO. 36—Wine skirt; white Pierrot-collar blouse (or jewel-neckline with flat pleated collar); ruby necklace, earrings, ring; wine vest; white hose; wine shoes.

COSTUME NO. 37—Wine skirt; taupe and wine printed blouse with separate matching bow tie; taupe vest; ruby earrings, bracelet and ring; wine hose; wine shoes.

COSTUME NO. 38—Wine skirt; white satin mandarin-collar blouse; pearl earrings, necklace, pin, ring and bracelet; wine hose; wine shoes.

COSTUME NO. 39—Wine skirt; pink blouse with separate matching bow; wine vest; ruby earrings, ring, bracelet; wine hose; wine shoes.

COSTUME NO. 40—Wine skirt; taupe ascot blouse; ruby earrings, pin, ring, bracelet; taupe hose; wine shoes.

The forty suggested costumes are listed only to acquaint you with the basic concept and need not be adhered to as written. There are other fabrics, other collar styles, and a long list of other color combinations. However, to get the most for the least, you would be better off, in the beginning at least, to work with a few base colors. Don't fall into the trap of jumping around, and don't fall into the trap of buying something only because you like it. Everything you buy should be used in more than one combination.

Keep Your Shape in Shape

I won't say that people with class are never fat; in fact, I can cite three heavy examples: Robert Morley, Sydney Greenstreet and Orson Welles, but they are exceptions. Successful people generally know that keeping their shape in shape is very much part of the game.

There are enough exercise and diet books around, and this book is not meant to be an encyclopedia, so I will just tell you how I manage to maintain my own weight and keep myself physically fit. Skiing, sailing, swimming, playing tennis and my way of eating help keep my weight, more or less, stable. My attitudes about drinking and smoking are not intended as a lecture; they are just what I do, perhaps explaining why in my seventy-eighth year I still enjoy a completely active life, physically, intellectually and culturally. I have condensed considerable experience and research into a few pages of down-to-earth advice.

I control my weight quite simply by having the same breakfast and lunch every day, thereby avoiding all tempta-

People with class care about keeping their shape in shape.
COLLECTION OF MR. AND MRS. DON ELLIOTT.

tion. Breakfast consists of half grapefruit or grapefruit juice, four pieces of dry Melba toast and hot water. Perhaps I should explain why I drink hot water instead of coffee, tea or Coke. My doctor insists that I drink eight glasses of water a day to avoid the possibility of kidney stones or bladder infections. I said that was no problem because I have three cups of tea for breakfast, lunch and dinner. The doctor said coffee and tea don't count because they are diuretics. He also told me to have a bran-type cereal once a day to minimize the possibility of cancer of the colon. I chose, with his permission, bran flakes, which are less intensive than All-Bran. Besides, bran flakes mix well with my lunch staple, tuna fish.

While I am at it, I might add one more health tip. If you are too young to take advantage of it now, think about it when you become older. After a certain age, sometimes in the fifties, sometimes in the sixties, the body can no longer absorb lactose—milk, cheese, ice cream, in fact, any dairy product.

I am distressed to say that two very high-priced Park Avenue doctors let me go through three unpleasant years of indigestion without establishing the cause of my malaise. I learned about it only through Jane Brody's column in *The New York Times*. I gave up ice cream, milk, yogurt and cottage cheese, and was cured immediately. When I think about it, I get angry; but, then, remembering that misunderstandings are an everyday part of living, I smile.

Back to my diet. Lunch consists of tuna fish (three ounces canned in water, not oil), mixed with low-calorie mayonnaise, lemon juice, and bran flakes, garnished either with lettuce and tomato and/or string beans, carrots, spinach, beets (only the low-calorie vegetables). Dessert will be an apple, pear or peach in season. Dry salt-free Melba toast and hot water finish the meal. Dinners consist of eating anything that is put before me, but no second helpings of main course or dessert. The most difficult problem was giving up my nightly forays into the ice box. I reduced them finally to one visit, and limited myself to fresh fruit or vegetables plus one or two slices of dry Melba toast.

In order to avoid temptation on those very few occasions when I dine at a restaurant (we don't go to restaurants unless we've been invited because I prefer eating in the peace and quiet of our own home or someone else's home), I don't look at the menu. I order consommé, fish or chicken and grapefruit or melon for dessert. The waiter is asked not to put bread and butter at my place. I may take either dry Melba toast or a roll instead of dessert. We have no chocolates in the house. My major weakness is ice cream, and in the summertime I used to stop at Carvel automatically. Now I drive by Carvel without giving it a thought—it's out! My weight problem is handled, more or less, by refusing to look at the wealth of food available and confining our own dishes at home to fish, chicken, salads and low-calorie vegetables. If you think this sounds dull, you wouldn't if you came to dinner. On the other hand, before I controlled my eating, I would overeat terribly and always suffered from indigestion, a most uncomfortable and unpleasant feeling, not to mention continuous feelings of guilt.

Unfortunately, I do have a pot belly. A pot belly, in case you don't know, sticks out below the waistline as opposed to a normal belly, which is located above the waistline. If I had known before what I know now, there would have been no pot belly. A pot belly results when the stomach muscles haven't been exercised. This may also be a result of pregnancy, which happens not to be one of my personal problems. However, there is a short exercise that will eliminate all possibilities of a pot belly if used *before* the pot belly develops. Once it develops, it is too late.

Dr. Robert Siffert, director of New York's Mount Sinai Hospital's orthopedic division, recommends this exercise. Lie on your back, bend your knees with your feet comfortably secured under a couch, inhale, tense your belly, raise yourself to a forty-five-degree angle, count five and lie back. Repeat ten times. Start with one and build up to ten over a two-month period. Build up the muscles slowly; otherwise you will damage your back. I know, because I did. Doing this sit-up exercise eliminates the possibility of a pot belly, strengthens the stomach muscles, and eliminates future lower back problems.

Back problems plague many adults, so here are some other ways to avoid strain on the back: When lifting heavy objects, go into a squat position with your knees bent, keep your back vertical, and lift the object by standing up. All the strain is taken by the legs, none by the back. Bent knees spread the lower vertebrae and diminish pressure on the nerves; so, when sitting, always keep one or both knees higher than your hips. When standing, try to have one foot raised; that's the reason most taverns have a rail.

Your physical health comes from a strong heart, according to Dr. Kenneth Cooper, an army captain whose book on aerobics was a nationally respected best seller. His tests, conducted on some five thousand enlisted men, indicate that a strong heart results only from exercise. It is the heart muscle that must be exercised. The exercise can be tennis, jogging, swimming, skiing or any other vigorous activity. The shortest and most convenient way to exercise the heart is twelve minutes of jogging three to four mornings a week. Try it in front of the television set to eliminate the boredom. A strong heart muscle pumps more oxygen with each breath. The oxygen is distributed through the bloodstream to every part of your body. It is the oxygen that is responsible for good health. Calisthenics, on the other hand, serve only to keep you limber and light on your feet. It will also encourage better posture. Try the Canadian Air Force exercises three mornings a week for about six minutes. It's all you need to keep limber. I recommend the paperback edition of the Canadian Air Force exercise manual. It explains in greater detail things you should know about taking proper care of that wonderful machine you were born with—your body.

While we're on the subject of health, I suggest you give serious consideration to cutting out cigarettes, pipes and cigars. Foreign films indicate that, surprisingly, cigarette smoking is still as common abroad as beer drinking is here. In contrast, cigarette smoking in America has become déclassé except, strangely enough, among high-school students and, to a lesser degree, college students, even though they have been thoroughly exposed to the facts about the risks of cancer. The average number of cigarette smokers among our dinner guests is now down to one in seven, from four in seven.

Recently, dinner guests have been asking permission to smoke cigarettes at the table. In the past only pipe smokers and cigar smokers asked for permission. Cigarette smoking is unhealthy and objectionable. It creates unpleasant odors on your breath, your clothes, your hair and your furniture. Finally, of course, it is said to be a cause of lung cancer, emphysema, heart attacks and strokes.

Should you want to give it up, I can tell you, as one who did, that it is possible but not easy. According to everything I have read, three out of four who try are not successful. There are four possibilities.

1. Give it up now, cold turkey, because that may be the easiest way.
2. Try a hypnotist.
3. Try the Smoke-Enders or the Petrie method, both behavior-modification programs.
4. Give it up when you get the first symptoms of emphysema, cancer, heart trouble, smoker's cough, or smoker's voice.

It is considered bad form to enter anyone's home or office with a lighted cigarette. If there is no ash tray on the desk of the person you are visiting, it is better not to smoke.

It is surprising that these few pages are all the information you need to keep your shape in shape and to keep yourself in good health; surprising when one considers the large number of adults who are now going through the agonizing and time-consuming exercise of running three to ten miles a day. Yet, according to the man who wrote the book, ten to twelve minutes three times a week will accomplish the same thing.

Many of my friends keep their hearts in shape by swimming laps summer and winter (how boring I would find that), while others regularly go to a gym three times a week (how boring I would find that too). Still others go to a fat farm once or twice a year at considerable expense but with very little long-range effect on their health.

Writing this section was difficult, difficult because, having already written two books on the subject, I was faced with the problem of what to leave out. On the other hand, I know how many enthusiastic friends I have made: Those who really read the rules and used them effectively.

Clothes do not make the man, or the woman; neither do good manners, but dressing well goes a long way toward making one feel better about oneself. And good manners make *other* people feel better.

So, now, let's move on to what you do, another way of saying how to cope *graciously* with life's never-ending problems.

4

What You Do:

A. HOW YOU LIVE YOUR LIFE
B. HOW YOU ENTERTAIN

I was thirty-four, healthy, divorced, relatively attractive, a self-made millionaire retired from the day to day management of my business, and miserable. You may notice too that I had not yet learned that my shirt cuffs should show.

RAY LEVITT

"By the time we've made it, we've had it."

—*Malcolm Forbes*

I WAS THIRTY-FOUR, a self-made millionaire, and retired from the day-to-day management of my business, a business that had been created out of my own head. I was young, healthy, divorced, and resonably attractive. I had just completed the first leg of my retirement venture, a six-month trip around the United States in my new Chrysler Imperial convertible.

And I was miserable, so miserable I went directly to a psychoanalyst. There I learned (among a few other less important things) how to introduce myself at a party. The doctor explains, "You walk up to anyone, extend your hand, and say, 'My name is Mortimer Levitt.'" If I didn't know this at the age of thirty-four, it is likely that other successful entrepreneurs may not know it either. If I had known then what I know now, I would not have needed two years of psychoanalysis. The following pages indicate some of the many other things I didn't know. And in this chapter we will look into the actual substance of class, meaning what you actually do day to day, by far the most important component of the class scale.

Your life, like my life, and everyone else's life, consists of what you do: your career, how you make a living, your leisure time activities, your premarital love life, your married love life, your aspirations, your intellectual interests, your social activities and your athletic activities. It is your life to live, the only one you will have, and it passes all too quickly.

Indeed, if you don't keep a calendar, you will discover that a great part of your life has slipped away beyond recall. As one gets older, one's memory falters. One forgets some of the many incidents that have enriched one's life. One even forgets some of the trials and tribulations that, surprisingly, one has managed to live through. A diary expresses your feelings; a calendar simply records the facts, and requires no literary skill. In addition to keeping a calendar, I suggest filing away invitations and programs (theater, concert, film, testimonial dinners, opera, sports, et cetera), with a line or two about the quality and content of the performance. Keeping such records has one other advantage. It documents your own growth from your own perspective, showing you where you were and how far you have come. One of the exciting things about life is evidence of the continuing process of maturing (not aging). In this sense, looking back can be rewarding regardless of the state in which you find yourself at a particularly unhappy moment.

After New York's Mayor Koch failed to win his party's gubernatorial nomination, he was interviewed on television by Gabe Pressman.

> PRESSMAN: "So, Mr. Mayor, are you any smarter now?"
>
> KOCH: "No, Gabe, not smarter, but wiser."

To enjoy life to the fullest presupposes two conditions: that you are in love; that you are productive.

Being in love doesn't mean simply to love, but to love and be loved in return. That sounds like the lyrics from Nat King Cole's golden single "Nature Boy." Few people are so lucky. Some never love at all. Some are loved, but only fleetingly. Some find it and lose it. However, love is not something over which one has any control; it's more like a roulette wheel, except that one gets a *much* better deal in roulette where the odds are only 38 to 1.

Film star Glenda Jackson said, "The important thing in acting is to be able to laugh and cry. If I have to cry, I think of my sex life. If I have to laugh, I think of my sex life." For many, love relationships produce a similar ambivalence.

But friendship is almost as valuable because friendship too enriches life, usually with no ambivalence. Make friends for the qualities you enjoy in people, and ignore those several qualities you may not enjoy. You can't remake people, and they can't remake you. Although you may be a perfectionist, people are not perfect. People are human, with the many frailties that implies. If you are lucky, you will find soul mates in both sexes. Soul mates have little to do with sex; they are those rare people to whom you really relate. You are not going to have many soul mates, but that doesn't mean shutting the others out.

Being productive means doing something that "turns you on," not necessarily in the way you earn a living, although that would surely be a plus. Unlike animals, man has an ego that needs to be satisfied. The elder son of a close friend doesn't need to work because his grandfather left him a trust fund that provides income enough to live a sixties lifestyle—certainly not the lifestyle of his well-fixed parents. Yet, as long as this young man doesn't work—and he says he doesn't *want* to work—he will never be happy because deep down his ego does demand that he produce. And this boy-man is *not* happy.

Jill wants to write fiction, Bob can't wait to get on the tennis court, Frank wants to win the Harvest Moon Ball Dance Contest, Judy the marathon, Helmuth won't rest until he gets a one-man show for his paintings, Rebecca wants to be a brain surgeon, et cetera. Everyone needs to do something well. If your career does not satisfy your ego needs, get involved with something outside your career. And the best way to find that other something is to sit down and think through the possibilities.

Unfortunately, most people *do* without going through the essential preliminary stage of thinking about *what* to do. When I was so miserable and went to an analyst, that, I suppose, was a positive action.

Last June Mimi and I were invited to a 6:30 dinner party at the home of some Greens Farms neighbors. It was a perfect June day, yet the twenty-four guests were gathered in the family room—bar, pool table, stereo and a low ceiling. It was quite uncomfortable: too many guests, too much smoke, and too much noise. By 7:00 I couldn't stand the noise or the smoke and after a feeble attempt to get someone to join me on the outside terrace (it overlooked a lovely lawn), I went out by myself. I wasn't being sociable, but inasmuch as I was drinking club soda and dinner was probably still an hour away, I used the time profitably. *I began to think.* And, soon, I was outlining much of this book on a small piece of paper; that is, I wrote down words representing the key ideas for the book's content and its four main divisions.

I might just as well have spent the same time jotting down possible new activities for the coming winter. (In a four-season climate, nature provides the chance to vary your lifestyle.) The simple act of *thinking and recording* one's thoughts paves the way for action. Ideas represent personal creativity and are too valuable to lose, especially when they touch upon new and potentially exciting directions. Routinely having a pen and a 3-x-5-inch index card on your person makes it easy to record ideas before they slip away. Putting the ideas on paper gives them a pot in which to simmer. For me, making notes is always the first step toward resolving any problem. Too often, people will not act until there is a crisis, and then they act hastily, without thinking.

Many people spend much of their leisure time doing the equivalent of nothing, that is, reading newspapers and watching television, instead of, perhaps, reading books or exchanging ideas with others.

"I do not take a single newspaper," said Thomas Jefferson, "nor read one once a month, and I feel myself infinitely the happier for it."

When you think about it, there is little real news in your morning newspaper. By real news I mean such things as Napoleon meeting his Waterloo; Martin Luther King's assassination; the dropping of the atom bomb on Hiroshima. Significant events of political, social and economic history are few and far between. The events of the day are largely human-interest stories—murders, rapes, scandals, swindles —plus sports and the stock market.

Americans frequently watch the news from 5 to 7 P.M., then catch it again a few hours later at 10 or 11 P.M., and again on the morning radio, and then read it (one more time) in the morning paper. The news, such as it is, becomes an excuse for wasting time. Albert Camus said: "A single sentence will suffice for modern man: he fornicated and read the newspaper." To which I would add "and watched most sports on television." In a recent column in the *New York Times*, Russell Baker described his own addiction to pro football:

> I slumped in my chair in the lowering stupors of Sunday afternoons and wallowed in fandom. I became part of that great monstrous organism, The Fans. What I really was, of course, was a jerk.

Reading books is a more fufilling activity than reading newspapers or watching television. Mark Twain said it very well, "The man who doesn't read books has no advantage over the man who can't read them." We give up the advantages of literacy when we do not exercise the skill.

Some might argue that they are too tired or too anxious to take up a book of an evening and that the passive act of television-watching is the best antidote for their condition. Let me divulge my two secrets for achieving relaxation, a relaxation that carries me through the day and the night and from the night into the day.

1. I do Transcendental Meditation for twenty minutes every morning. I am not confirming the many claims made for it by the experiments conducted at Harvard University, one conclusion being that twenty minutes of TM is the equivalent of two hours of sleep; I really don't believe it. On the other hand, as presented, it seems to be quite legitimate. Regardless, I find TM to be a good way to start my day feeling refreshed and relaxed. TM has become an international phenomenon, and a program can usually be found by consulting your phone book.

2. Instead of the usual six o'clock cocktail, I sleep. Every day before dinner, from 6:15 to 7:00 P.M., I take all my clothes off and get into bed. I wake up by myself— no alarm—completely refreshed. I wash and come down to dinner in a floor-length robe feeling comfortable and elegant. If we are going out, we dress between 7:00 and 7:30 P.M. On those rare occasions when I go out directly from the office, I take my nap there. Long ago Mimi gave me a special couch for the office, perfect for stretching out full length. Nothing ever gets in the way of my before-dinner sleep. That daily nap gives me, in effect, two days for the price of one. That is, I have a daytime day and, after my nap, a nighttime day. On the very rare occasions when I don't have forty-five minutes to nap, I meditate a second time because it takes only twenty minutes.

I consider entertaining at home to be the single most important aspect of my personal life. You might be shy

A full life includes recreational sports not *necessarily skiing.*
COLLECTION OF THE AUTHOR.

about entertaining, but I urge you to try it nonetheless. In any case, there are additional ways to lead an active life. Sports provide one obvious distraction. I began playing golf in 1932. It frustrated me for nineteen years. One day, out of the blue, in 1952, I shot an 82. Before that, 91 was my best. I said, "Mimi, I'll never play golf again! I will not spend the rest of my life trying to equal that score." I gave my clubs away, and switched to tennis. Happy, happy day!

I switched from golf to tennis at an age when other men switch from tennis to golf. As I go to the office only one day a week in the summer, I had to find tennis companions. Mimi had switched from tennis to golf when she was very, very young. She was a club champion three times; so, she was hardly a candidate for tennis. The result was that I became the Bobby Riggs of Westport. Here's how that happened.

To begin with, during the week there were few men available because men were working, and properly so. On the few occasions I played with men, I discovered they were too fast and too erratic. In contrast, the women I played with were steadier, slower, and hit the kind of balls that were easier to return. In 1968 I became the self-appointed mixed singles champion of Westport by beating the woman singles champion. There are twenty-seven women on my tennis list, but I have no set dates. When I am playing well, I telephone the better players; when my game goes off, I preserve my ego by phoning the women who don't play that well.

Now, being in my seventy-eighth year, I spend part of the time talking; that is, I rest after every four games. Sometimes the conversation is just as much fun as the tennis. You may be interested to know why I don't play doubles. There are four reasons:

1. I must be prepared to return every ball, but by the law of averages, only one ball in two comes to my side of the court. I abhor wasted labor, meaning I dislike the idea of preparing for balls that will never come to me.

2. I become embarrassed if my partner is playing well and scoring hard-to-make shots that I lose because I am playing badly.

3. The reverse is equally true, except that I don't become embarrassed, I become exasperated.

4. It is easier to get one player than three.

When the time comes that I can no longer play singles, I will give up the game; but assuredly it will be replaced with another activity.

Arts and crafts are a logical choice for using time productively, especially for those with an artistic bent. Photography comes to mind as perhaps the art form most readily accessible, and one I returned to after a long hiatus.

I stopped taking photographs about thirty years ago, after our fifty-four-week honeymoon to Europe and the Middle East. Thereafter, the only pictures I took were those recording the birthdays of our two children. They were sent out as Christmas cards every year. Then, in May 1982, Anthony Bergamo, executive vice-president of the Custom Shops, gave me a camera, a Minolta with automatic focus and automatic light meter. And to my great surprise, I began taking pictures again. Because it's hard to miss a shot with the camera he gave me, I bring it along whenever we visit, and take pictures of everything and everyone. I mail them out as thank-you notes or souvenirs. I take only closeups, three and a half to four feet away, in color. I take portraits only in open shade, *never* in direct sunlight. I take few flash pictures because flash lighting flatters no one, unless the flash is bounced off the ceiling.

I'm ashamed to say I've dumped my own thousand or so snapshots into a corrugated box (for now), yet I know that when I can no longer play tennis, sail, ski, and am no longer productive at the office, I'll pass many nostalgic hours pasting my snaps into sequential albums. I'll look back and dream; then, from time to time, I will take out the many slides and home movies we took in the days when photography was both a hobby and a recording of our life. In my own case, there was, in addition to my calendar, a diary, but one which, frankly, is too painful to look at. My guess is that yours might be equally painful because life is, so frequently, a vale of tears.

Community affairs provide another outlet that can be both useful and soul-satisfying. Mimi has always been a participant. She was an active member of the PTA for the Town School, the elementary school attended by both our children. She did a major job in helping to raise funds so the school could enlarge its facilities. Later when our son Peter went to Trinity School, Mimi was active on its behalf. As a volunteer, Mimi taught remedial reading in a Harlem elementary school. She organized and became president of the Eighty-second Street Neighborhood Association, and helped to maintain the quality of the area adjacent to the Metropolitan Museum, an area which was finally declared an historic district. Although Mimi is not on the board of Young Concert Artists or on the board of the Levitt Pavilion for the Performing Arts, her efforts on behalf of both organizations were just as productive. Unlike me, Mimi takes elections for political office seriously. So, whenever I vote, Mimi gives me a list of the people I should vote for, and I do exactly as she suggests, except that is, for the president, governor or mayor. There Mimi and I are not always in agreement, in which case I say, "Let's not vote because we cancel each other out." Mimi says, "Mortimer, you are not obliged to vote, but I appreciate living in a country where my vote counts, and I'm voting. You do what you like."

So, even though I'm not enthusiastic about it, I vote too.

This brings me to charitable contributions. As one moves up the economic ladder, one becomes bombarded by requests for contributions. Most causes are worthwhile, so how does one decide who gets and who doesn't? No matter how much money you have, there is never really enough. One solution is so easy it's hard to understand why it took me so long to learn it. You give because a friend is working for that cause. In other words, you give within your means, but not to the cause; rather, you give to your friend because it has become, for whatever reason, his cause. Even more important, become involved yourself because the need is infinite. Find a cause that turns you on, and you will be rewarded.

The point of all of the above is that people who rate high on our class scale are people who make the most of their time, who do useful and interesting things that bring them into touch with other people, and who create situations for enhancing life whenever life does not automatically bestow such favors on them.

Pursuit of a career, a consuming hobby, or a recreational activity should make up a large part of what you do. Among the sports you might consider are tennis, golf, handball, racquetball, squash, horseback riding, swimming, sailing, softball, skiing. As for hobbies, consider photography, gardening, sculpting, painting, drawing, cooking, sewing, reading, taking courses, traveling, sightseeing, visiting museums. There is no end to the hobbies and sports available to the enterprising. But regardless of the degree of your success in those areas, nothing will enrich your life more effectively than entertaining regularly.

The Pleasures and Rewards
of Entertaining at Home

Viewed from a blimp, the crowd watching the Rose Bowl game looks like colored grains of sand placed in a land-locked bowl, yet each grain represents a unique person whose problems, while completely different from your own, are paradoxically almost the same. As Gracie Allen said, "People really are more interesting than anybody," and the best way to enjoy their individuality is to invite them to a small dinner party.

Entertaining at home is particularly meaningful to me because in the home where I grew up we never entertained. I can remember only two parties. The first was for grownups: I have no idea what the occasion was, but I was permitted to stay up even though I was only four or five. One guest, a friend of my aunt Rose, played Scott Joplin type music on our piano. I fell in love with the piano that night and have been in love with it ever since. The second party was in the afternoon, a celebration for my sixth birthday. I vividly remember playing musical chairs. There was one other—a tea party. I must have been eight, when two of Mother's friends unexpectedly arrived at our house one afternoon. Mother was due shortly, so I asked the ladies to stay. I set a table and served them tea. As I write this, it doesn't seem possible, but I know for sure that it actually did happen. Obviously, I was born to be a host.

Polly Adler, New York City's famous madam, wrote a best seller called *A House Is Not a Home*. I would amend

Polly's title to say that a house is not a home unless it has books, music, paintings, and, above all, people—first, last, and always, people. People are endlessly interesting, and entertaining is the main way to exchange life's experiences. Entertaining really is the one thing you *can* do to enrich your life regardless of circumstances. Yet most people do *not* entertain regularly. And those who entertain at all are more apt to have one or two big cocktail parties (or buffets) a year, but only to discharge their own social obligations.

You can (and should) entertain no matter what your circumstances. Bringing people together is fun. There is no need for servants or champagne. People enjoy making themselves a drink; and the bar is a convenient place to say hello. Entertaining enhances one's sense of living well. People supply the substance; your imagination supplies the style. Luxury is dependent only upon style in relation to your purse. If funds are limited, spend only half the money you have saved for a vacation trip; use the other half for entertaining. Entertaining will also enlarge your circle of friends and acquaintances.

We have friends with all the appurtenances of the good life—a large country home with a New York pied-à-terre, a Rolls-Royce or Mercedes, a condominium in Palm Beach, Palm Springs or the Caribbean, and the necessary money to take vacations around the world. Not long ago, one such friend invited us to a dinner party weeks in advance. As I had already begun to schedule a dinner party for that night (and as we were very close friends), I asked if she could change to the next day or the following Saturday. "No," she replied, "I have booked Marie for that night and Marie is hard to get." These friends who live in such splendor depend upon the inflexible schedule of a free-lance cook. Actually, they seldom entertain at home. Instead, they take friends to expensive restaurants, usually noisy and crowded, where the food seldom equals the quality one can achieve at home.

I am fortunate indeed to have Mimi as a hostess. Though she had no prior training, she was a natural. Mimi was born in Vienna of well-to-do parents, came to the States when she was eighteen and was graduated Phi Beta Kappa from Pomona College. She joined the staff of New York's Museum of Modern Art, becoming secretary to the Permanent Collection under the direction of Alfred Barr. At the time I met Mimi she was recently back with the museum after having taken a one-year leave of absence to become head of a translating section at the main Nuremberg trials.

Mimi had no interest in clothes other than being certain she was never overdressed. When we were first married, she frequently left the house without wearing lipstick. Even today it takes me longer to dress.

Before I took over from Mimi the complicated task of setting up two dinner parties a week, I hadn't realized how much time was involved. Mimi explained that she could not telephone a friend and simply invite her to dinner. She had, first, to ask after the children, the in-laws, the school problem, etc. If it was near election time, they had to talk about that too, the result (for Mimi) being that inviting friends had become a chore rather than a pleasure. One day I said, "Mimi, woman's work is never done; let me handle the inviting." She was pleased, but skeptical.

Anyway, I made the job much less time-consuming by having my secretary telephone husbands at their offices rather than calling wives, as the husbands' calendars had to be cleared anyway. In addition, there is always someone at the office.

Arranging a good dinner party may not be an art, but it does require some thinking. It is not advisable, for example, to invite two lawyers, two producers, two architects, or two stockbrokers because you may find them talking shop to the exclusion of other guests. Artists of any kind usually make desirable guests: painters, composers, playwrights, authors, directors and designers. Lawyers always have stories to tell about cases that are interesting, amusing, or both.

In the course of entertaining, to what extent does one act as a matchmaker? Proust said that "one of a hostess's duties is to act as a procuress," and in this day and age, with the social scene flooded with singles, it is difficult not to contemplate the general question.

My own experience suggests that a certain discretion is usually the best tactic in bringing together a pair whom you visualize as being suited to each other.

At the time I suggested that we reduce our dinner parties from eight people to six, Mimi warned me that a last-minute cancellation would upset any well-planned evening. But there were no such cancellations for a while. Finally, it did happen. A medical emergency at six o'clock caused one couple to cancel. I said to Mimi, "Let me handle it."

I made twelve phone calls, but got no one to fill in. So, here we were down to four. Our female guest was chairman of one of the country's most prestigious specialty stores. Our male guest was chairman of an important optics conglomerate. They were both recently divorced, and it was slightly embarrassing, there being no other guests. Much too obvious. I seemed to be pointing out that they were in the market for a partner, a friend and maybe a spouse. Such matchmaking efforts should properly take place at a larger gathering. Much to Mimi's surprise, however, the four of us had a wonderful time. I distinctly remember that the evening did not break up until a few minutes past midnight. Despite the pleasant evening the four of us enjoyed, there was no follow-up. I learned later that his heart had already been lost to the woman he subsequently married.

Years ago, when our children were growing up, Mimi gave tree-trimming parties at Christmas and made it a practice to invite our many single friends. On one such occasion I especially wanted two of them to meet: David Brockman and an exotic Russian beauty with the temperament of an opera star, Elizabeth de Seversky. David is handsome and virile with white hair and a craggy face. Elizabeth is one of the most imaginative women we have ever known and a particularly devoted friend, especially if there is trouble. In fact, Elizabeth has a penchant for finding friends who are in trouble, and there is no limit to what she will do to help. It so happened that David was busy that night, but I insisted that he come by, and he did, late. He then made the mistake of paying attention to another woman. I took him aside and said, "David, that's the wrong one. This one is Elizabeth, and be sure to take her home." He did, and a year later they were married! And during the twenty stormy years since, I have been alternately blessed and blamed for bringing them together.

On still another occasion, I invited an attractive fifty-seven-year-old widower with five children and a good-looking woman of forty-one who had recently separated from her second husband. At first glance it appeared to be a meeting arranged in heaven. She was president of a nature center in Darien, Connecticut, and Bill was one of Greenwich's wealthiest sportsmen. Almost immediately after dinner Nancy whispered to me, "Can you imagine a man who enjoys *killing* deer and birds for fun?" That evening was a disaster.

Mixing people is usually great fun. And then there are those very special occasions that require a great deal of planning. I'll tell you about some of them.

Chamber Theater Party

I was a founding member of New York's Manhattan Theater Club; Bob Sickinger was the artistic director. Bob came to New York from Chicago where he had conceived the idea of chamber theater (play readings by professional actors in private homes). Those evenings usually started with beer and pretzels.

I suggested to Mimi that it might be fun to host such an evening. She agreed, then added her own touch. A black-tie, sit-down dinner for forty people followed the reading. The play was *Monkey in a Cage* by Venable Herndon. Most of our living-room furniture was removed, and folding chairs set up theater style. Our six actors were perched on bar stools. Two spotlights had been positioned for the actors, who wore light makeup to conceal normal city pallor.

After the reading, Herndon led an animated discussion of the play. Listening to our friends made it easier to understand the usual differences among theatrical critics. After cocktails in the library, our guests went down to the dining room. There were four tables of eight, and a fifth table of eight in the foyer. Our friend, Enid Nemy, a feature writer for the *New York Times*, unexpectedly brought a photographer along. A half-page story on the evening, complete with photographs, appeared in the Sunday *Times*.

Good-Bye Party

Mimi gave a black-tie good-bye party for Edith and Marty Segal. Marty was taking a six-month sabbatical, and they intended to spend most of their time in Paris because Marty is a Sunday painter. There were forty-eight guests, all mutual friends. The party began with cocktails in the library followed by dinner downstairs in our dining room and terrace. The living room had been closed off, and a sign was affixed to the living-room doors:

> "Chez Mimi"
> A partir de 22:00 heures

Mimi served a typical French menu with vintage Bordeaux and champagne. Once again Mimi had removed the furniture from our living room. This time the room was transformed into a bistro. A typical Parisian news vendor's stall was built in one corner of the room and served as a bar. Small round marble-top tables, a dance floor, and small wire-back chairs were rented. Original French posters from present-day Paris were hung on the walls, and bon-voyage balloons hung inside and outside our home. The Segals were being sent off in style.

Birthday Party

One Monday afternoon when I returned home from the office, the dining-room door was closed. Mimi greeted me by saying the second floor was off limits, that I should dress in formal clothes and that we were having friends in for dinner. I had no idea who was coming. Friends began to arrive at 7:30. By 8:15 there were some forty-five people in our library having cocktails. Mimi flicked the lights on and off, which I took as a signal to go downstairs for dinner. To my great surprise she opened the doors to the living room. It had been set up theater style. Guests received an actual Playbill with my caricature on the cover done by Hirschfeld. The program read: "One-time-only Productions presents 'An Evening with Mortimer.'" Michael Brown, a close friend and a longtime theatrical producer, co-produced the fifty-five-minute show with Mimi and Manya Starr, another longtime friend, who writes for films and TV. Michael acted as emcee. The Playbill noted that "this production was made possible by an unsuspecting grant from Mortimer Levitt." Manya read aloud birthday telegrams she had written from world-famous celebrities; they were hilarious. Charles Wadsworth, concert pianist and artistic director of the Chamber Music Society of Lincoln Center, did two numbers at the piano: the first was a take-off on Jimmy Carter, and the other was a special birthday song composed for the occasion. Harold Rome

PLAYBILL

LEVITT THEATRE

An Evening With Mortimer

Entertaining may be simple or elaborate, but an element of thoughtfulness is essential.

did two numbers from shows he had written that were particularly appropriate to the occasion. Barbara Carroll, one of America's great popular pianists, sent a birthday tape of a special song written by Michael. Norma French, a leading soprano with the New York City Opera Company, sang two arias suited to the occasion. The show wound up with a slide presentation, a roast, based on snapshots that Mimi had dug up from an available thousand. A gala sit-down dinner followed.

Pre-Election Party

Mr. and Mrs. Larry Lachman (he is the former chairman of the board of Bloomingdale's) invited us to dinner. His wife Judy opened the door, and looking over her shoulder I could see into the library, where most of the guests were having cocktails. I said to Judy, "My goodness, am I really *that* old?" I don't have gray hair and still play singles and ski, so it was a shock to realize that her guests reflected my age group although some were younger.

The party took on a special character when, after dinner, we moved to the living room. Larry assembled the guests in a large circle. It was late spring, and the year of a presidential election. Larry, acting as moderator, asked each guest, in turn, whom they would favor for the Republican nomination. Bush turned out to be the number one choice. The entire after-dinner conversation stayed on that one subject because Larry handled it so well. Everyone had equal opportunity to be heard. It is the kind of evening we usually have with six; however, in our case, the conversation shifts from person to person and generally centers around each guest's current activity.

Magic Party

On my seventy-second birthday there was no surprise party although there were eighteen people for dinner. After dinner, however, Mimi said, "I have a little surprise for all of you; let's take the elevator to the fourth floor." Our fourth floor has two large bedrooms, originally one for each child. The children were no longer living at home, and Mimi was in the process of converting both rooms into guest rooms. The rooms had been completely stripped, so I could not imagine what we would be doing on the fourth floor. The entrance to the room facing the garden had been enclosed with a tent-like structure and a flap entrance in green felt. Inside, the lighting created an atmosphere that one might find upon entering a room in which a séance was going to be held. Eighteen high-backed bar stools were arranged in a large semicircle. Facing the semicircle, about two feet in front of the wall, was a half-moon table covered in matching green felt.

Mimi made an announcement. "On this very special occasion, I have the honor to present a very special magician, the elusive Mandami, guaranteed to mystify, guaranteed to amuse." Like a rabbit pulled out of a top hat, a magician entered seemingly from nowhere. Actually, he had been spirited away in the front bedroom, but I had no idea how he got there without my knowing. He performed his magic between the wall and the green table, having no paraphernalia at all except a tiny bag the size doctors carry. Mandami seemed to produce everything but elephants. For a magician to work so many miracles at such close range was mystifying indeed, and, as Mimi suggested, it was done with grace, humor, imagination and enormous skill. It was another evening on which I could only wonder at Mimi's ingenuity and, to me, her continual thoughtfulness: she knows I love magicians.

A Party at the Plaza

We received an engraved invitation from Ronald Revere to a surprise party for his wife, Joanna. It turned out to be a black-tie dinner dance, in celebration of Joanna's fortieth birthday. Ronald had 385 guests filling the Grand Ballroom of the Plaza. A gourmet dinner, the Plaza's best, was served, complete with vintage wines, white and red, and Dom Perignon champagne. There was a twenty-two-piece orchestra, led by Michael Carney. Carney played until midnight. At 11:30 a smaller room opened and a live disco band played for the young and the young-at-heart. It was as lavish a surprise party as any man could give to his wife, although it did lack intimacy.

My Surprise Party

Now, having observed Mimi's talent at close range, you might think that I would have learned enough to arrange a party for Mimi. Unfortunately, I just don't seem to have that kind of imagination; and in all the years I surprised Mimi only once. I told her that Glenn Bernbaum had invited us to dine with him at Mortimer's. Although I don't own Mortimer's, here's how it happens to bear my name. Glenn Bernbaum was executive vice-president of the Custom Shop and was its active head for twenty years. He is a bachelor and a brilliant cook. When he decided to open a restaurant while still running the Custom Shops, he named it after me. Mortimer's is an "in" restaurant for the beautiful people, not because of the name, but because Glenn is also an excellent administrator and a charming host.

It was Mimi's birthday, and when we arrived, Glenn greeted us at the door. As we were saying hello, Mimi said, "Oh, look, there's Mack Lipkin [a very close friend]. What's he doing here?" She excused herself to say hello to Mack, and as she approached the table she realized that I had brought together three of her favorite couples. This one time it was Mimi's turn to go white.

Though these evenings were indeed memorable, I do not want to leave you with the impression that one's normal entertaining must be conducted on a grand scale. It is not necessary to compete with friends who have larger incomes and there is no need to overspend.

There are many different ways to entertain, some relatively inexpensive: a buffet for twelve to twenty—salad, pasta and a jug of California red wine. Throw in coffee and Schnecken. On another occasion you can be sure of making guests happy with a frankfurter and beer party: garnish with sauerkraut/potato salad/pickles.

People love both caviar *and* pasta: the important difference is the preparation, the presentation and the guest mixture.

If you have the energy—and you should, because entertaining is so rewarding—there are many occasions that call for special parties: Valentine's Day, election day, graduation day, and Mother's Day. And there are parties for watching major events—Super Bowl, Kentucky Derby, the Oscars, the Emmys, the Miss America finals, etc. or the viewing of an opera or a much-heralded TV special. There are also anniversary parties, birthday parties, a welcoming party for new neighbors, a bon voyage party for departing friends, a community party (where the hostess provides the main course, and others provide the hor d'oeuvres and desserts).

Remember, your guests will be more comfortable if *you* are comfortable with your approach to entertaining. Your own personality, reflected in the warmth of your home, your friends and good conversation, draws guests back to your table.

I mentioned earlier that six is the ideal number—host and hostess plus two other couples. During our first few years of entertaining, we were always eight. I realized that conversation was fragmented, more chitchat than conversation, and guests tended to leave early, as early as 10:00 P.M. When I cut back to six, our evenings became more interesting, and guests frequently stay until midnight.

The most unsatisfying parties occur with tables of ten or twelve, unfortunately the invitation one is most apt to receive. They are difficult because, for the most part, conversation is confined only to the person on your right and the person on your left. Difficult also because if you should get into a deeply interesting conversation with the person on your right, you tend to ignore the person on your left. You can't do that without offending both that person and your hostess (who will be watching).

Most sit-down dinner parties are for twelve because labor costs for the outside help hired for the occasion are the same for eight, ten, or twelve. Any number over twelve requires only one or two extra staff for serving and cleaning up.

If circumstances are such that you are obliged to invite twelve, try two tables of six, and have the men switch tables for dessert. By the time dinner is finished, everyone will have had a chance to visit with everyone else. And, if the hostess had done her part in briefing her guests, the evening will have been even more enjoyable.

It is desirable to use place cards when seating guests at large parties for two reasons: (1) It saves them the embarrassment of deciding where or with whom they want to sit; and (2) Most important, you know your guests, and you can make the evening more pleasurable by grouping together those who are most apt to be compatible.

How to Be a Guest with Class

An invitation to a party or for a weekend sets off a reaction that involves the guest in more than merely accepting the invitation. Guests are remembered fondly and warmly because of their contribution to the evening as well as for their thoughtfulness to the hosts. Ideally, one should:

- Acknowledge an invitation promptly.
- Ask what kind of evening it is to be so that one may dress properly.
- Never cancel unless it is a true emergency.
- Write or phone your hostess the next day.

However, we do not live in an ideal society, and I sense more and more a deterioration in the thoughtfulness of guests, particularly in New York. Enid Nemy recently devoted an entire *New York Times* column to the increasing trend toward last-minute cancellations.

Here, then, are a few suggestions of do's and don'ts for the guest:

Parties
• Arrive no more than fifteen minutes late for a dinner party.
• Be considerate about putting glasses down on wood tables.
• Mingle with the other guests, remembering you have been invited specifically for that reason.
• Depending on the occasion, a small gift to indicate your thoughtfulness—flowers, wine, a gourmet treat or any small token that might add a nice note—is appreciated.
• Offer to help the hostess but if she declines, don't insist.
• Leave at a proper time—not too early or too late. Watch your host for a clue.
• If you wish to bring someone to a party, be sure to clear it first with the hostess. Normally, it is no problem if the event is a cocktail party, but a dinner party is usually structured, and an extra person may present a problem.
• Let the host or hostess approach you at parties—don't seek them out. They are busy and should get around to all the guests, but they shouldn't be hogged even if they are the only ones you know at the party.
• Send a thank-you note (not a bought card) the next day, or telephone. When people have a party, they always like to hear that their guests enjoyed it.

If thoughtfulness doesn't come naturally, make the effort to develop it. Thoughtfulness gives one a sense of sharing life. Thoughtfulness means a positive involvement. Send flowers, bring gifts, make phone calls, and by all means

"Get a grip on yourself, Grace. Somebody left them on the bus." Be gracious. Bring flowers.

write thank-you notes. You will feel better about yourself for having taken the trouble.

Weekends

- If you fail to bring a gift, plan to send one after you leave, based on observations of things your hosts might appreciate for their home.

- If there are no servants, make your own bed; then ask your hostess about stripping the bed when you leave.
- If you are an early riser, discuss that with your hostess the night before, and arrange to make your own coffee in the morning.
- If you want to go off by yourself or with your companion, don't hesitate to say so to the hosts—then make your own arrangements. One problem with weekend guests is that both hosts and guests feel obligated to spend 100 percent of the time together. On the other hand, be sure to clear any departure with your hosts first and don't make your own plans independently.
- Offer to help with the work in a home with no servants, and insist on doing your share.
- If there *are* servants, tip them generously when you leave. That makes it easier for your hostess to invite guests again because the help is pleased to earn the extra money.
- If you have not been to the home before, comment on the things you like—the art, an accessory, an antique, etc.
- If the hosts have an outside event to attend while you are there that does not include you, do not get upset; and assure your hosts that you will be perfectly fine while they are gone.
- Take an active role in the weekend; offer to cook a special dish, or take photographs of the group, or take your hosts out to lunch or dinner.
- Take your cue from your hosts: if they like to retire early, go along.

How to Create a Friendly Atmosphere in Your Home

Since entertaining at home is so important to living a full life, it seems appropriate to give serious thought to the environment in which the entertainment takes place. There are many ways to create a warm and comfortable setting for conversation with friends, and these fit any budget. No matter how much or how little money is spent on decorating your home, four elements that give an impression of civilized living are always the same: pictures, books, music and plants.

Hang Pictures

Walls should be covered with pictures that are tastefully framed and properly hung. They need not be oil paintings. Watercolors, engravings, lithographs, posters and reproductions fill the need just as well. The Metropolitan Museum of Art and Lincoln Center both have an extraordinary collection of really handsome posters for only $9, and they can be framed for as little as $20. These are posters that would add warmth to any setting. The important thing is that you have given some thought to the content, to the framing, and to the wall arrangement.

Like anything else, there is a trick to hanging pictures. Hang your pictures as low as possible if you want the feeling of their being in the room rather than on the wall. The bottom of the picture should be about forty-two inches from the floor. It could be an inch or two higher or

"Aren't you lucky! Very few people have anything original that's nice."

A friendly home needs paintings, etchings, drawings or posters on the walls.

COLLECTION OF THE AUTHOR.

lower depending on the furniture and size of the picture. If there are multiple pictures, lay them out on the floor before hanging them on the wall. It's easy to compose a good arrangement on the floor, easy to keep rearranging them until they look just right. Once you feel that you can't do any better, leave them on the floor for twenty-four hours. If they look just as good the next day, you have hit the bull's-eye.

Add Books

Bookshelves should indicate not only that books are bought, but also that these books are read. One doesn't need a wall full of books; a few shelves of interesting titles reflecting your personal taste are sufficient.

Add Music

A quality stereo system discreetly installed indicates an appreciation of music. As a result of considerable testing, psychologists have learned that to be appreciated music must be turned off. If music is on all the time, one no longer hears it; worse, it is wearing on the nerves. If music is turned off from time to time, one hears it when it goes back on. Then, it can create a pleasant background for other activities.

It is desirable to have music playing when your guests are arriving. Easy-listening music is obviously programmed for background music, but I have another suggestion: try classical music. It creates a more inviting reception. However, it cannot be a Beethoven symphony or Wagnerian opera; the piano music of Chopin or Schumann is easy to listen to and is quite beautiful. Try Chopin's preludes,

"*Oh, here's Mortimer, home from work. Gertrude, put 'Chariots of Fire' on the record-player.*"

A friendly ambiance in the home also calls for music.

ballades, and/or Schumann's Kinderszenen. Once your guests have assembled, however, the music should be turned off. It is not an aid to conversation. But it does help to lighten the awkwardness early arrivals sometimes feel on entering a home.

Interior Decorating without Heartaches

If you are redoing your home and can afford to work with a decorator, there is an easy way to avoid the major disappointments that often result when the decorator shows the client a rendering—an elaborate (and costly) water-color done in perspective. A rendering is misleading, like the drawing one sees of a dress in a fashion magazine. You can save money and, even more important, heartache by following this suggested step-by-step approach.

Tell your decorator the general feeling you want. This could be based on a photograph or photographs you have gathered or a favorite piece of furniture in your home or the home of a friend. In other words, *you* must have a starting place: Americana, French Provincial, Art Deco, Contemporary or whatever. Your own taste is the only criterion because you will be living with it. The objective is to create a room that pleases you.

After establishing the theme, decide on a color scheme based upon a favorite fabric, a photograph or an existing room. Then decide on your budget.

The decorator will first make a floor plan. If you like that, he will then shop the market alone and select the furniture he recommends. He will bring you photos or send you out on your own to see the things he has chosen.

You may bring him a few alternate pieces that you would like illustrated in his elevations.

If his selections meet with your approval, he will draw an elevation to scale for every wall in the rooms he is doing. Elevations include furniture, lamps, pictures, drapes, moldings, if any, etc. It is less expensive to change your mind on paper by having him draw in something you might like better. The decorator will draw it on a separate piece of transparent paper so you can see it in an overlay. Once you have bought a piece of furniture, it's yours. Therefore, draw everything first. You actually see it, in scale, in place, before you buy it. If your decorator can't draw elevations, don't use him because you are sure to make expensive mistakes.

A well-decorated home should have a lived-in quality. The mistake some decorators make with wealthy clients is to design a period room. As the old joke goes, "this room is so beautiful, it's to drop dead, period!" If the decorator hasn't achieved a comfortable lived-in look, you have missed the boat no matter how much you've spent.

Use Lighting that Makes People Look Good

Warm, friendly lighting is obviously needed for the ambiance you are trying to create. Each corner of the room should have its own lamp or area of indirect lighting. Light bulbs should always be shaded, especially the bulbs on wall sconces and chandeliers. Light-colored floors, carpets and walls make people look better, and a friendlier atmosphere results. In contrast, dark colors draw color from the face and create a rather stark atmosphere. A comfortable chair for reading needs its own special reading lamp alongside.

Touches of Class around the House
- Place fine soap in the powder room.
- Use linen towels instead of paper towels.
- Use linen napkins and linen tablecloths.
- Try matching coat hangers.
- Shield light bulbs in guest closets.
- Vary your dinner dishes for each course instead of using only matched sets.
- Have fresh flowers or plants throughout your home.
- Arrange the lighting so that it flatters both food and guests.
- If you have a servant, provide a uniform—a white jacket for the man, a black dress with white collar and cuffs for the woman.
- If you have a servant, have the guest's bed turned down at night.
- Keep facial tissues in a Lucite container.
- Avoid plastic place mats even for informal occasions.
- When guests leave, see them to the door.

Touches of Class at the Table
- Your dinner table is enhanced by candles.
- A centerpiece of fresh flowers should not block anyone's view of the diners. Unless you are an expert at floral arrangements, I suggest using flowers of one color only.
- Etiquette says that ashtrays be placed on the table; however, as a way of discouraging smoking during the meal, we no longer put cigarettes or ashtrays on the table.

Everybody eats, but not everyone knows how to eat gracefully. Some years ago, a reporter, having been assigned to do a story on Emily Post, was invited to her home for lunch. Feelings nervous, he had two martinis before arriving, thinking that he would not be offered cocktails. But, in fact, she offered him not only a martini, but wine with lunch. While he was cutting a lamb chop, the knife slipped, and the chop sailed off the table into Emily Post's lap. After two seconds of mortified silence, he said, "Well, you wrote the book . . . what do I do now?" She suggested, politely, that he go home and return at a future date.

Because poor table manners are unattractive, I offer the following do's and don'ts, some of which I too picked up along the way.

- When using silverware, start with the outside pieces and work your way in as the courses progress.
- Lean over the table slightly each time you take a bite to avoid spilling food on yourself. Dogs lower their mouths to their food. People raise food to the mouth.
- When eating soup, tip the plate slightly away from you, and fill the spoon by moving it away, not toward you. Soup served in a cup may also be drunk by lifting the cup by the handles.
- All food is served from your left side. Take the serving fork in your left hand, the serving spoon in your right. Serve yourself; then place the fork and spoon side by side on the platter, fork on the left, spoon on the right.
- Europeans have a more graceful style of eating than Americans. Americans cut a piece of meat, put down the knife, transfer the fork from the left hand to right, spear

the piece of meat and bring it to the mouth. Europeans cut the meat and lift it to the mouth with the fork in the left hand. It has been said that when the pilgrims came into their bountiful harvests they ate so quickly that a pilgrim father introduced the American style of eating to slow them down. Europeans do eat more gracefully than Americans and I suggest you try the European style.

- Do not hold the fork in your left hand while drinking water.
- When the course is finished, place the knife and fork side by side on the plate.
- Break bread with your fingers; do not cut it. The butter knife is placed across the butter plate.
- Don't talk with your mouth full. Take small bites, and chew with your mouth closed. Quietly.
- Don't eat with your elbows on the table.
- Food platters are passed left to right.
- Squeeze a piece of lemon with your right hand, using your left hand as a shield to protect the person next to you.
- When ice cubes are left in your glass, do not chew the ice.
- Eat a cherry tomato whole, and be sure to keep your mouth closed when you bite into it.
- When not eating, keep your hands in your lap or rest your hands and wrists only on the table.
- Place your napkin on the left side of your plate when the meal is over. If plates have been removed, leave the napkin in the center.
- When passing your plate for second helpings, leave the knife and fork on the plate.

- It is permissible to sop up gravy with bread by putting a small piece down into the gravy, and then eating it with your fork.
- Asparagus may be eaten with the fingers if the tip is hard. But it may also be eaten with a fork.
- If bacon is limp, it should be eaten with a fork; but crisp, it may be picked up with the fingers.
- Clams and oysters on the half shell are speared with the small shellfish fork, dipped into the sauce, and eaten in one bite.
- Chicken and lamb chops are eaten with knife and fork. Only in family groups should they be picked up.
- Shrimp, if not too large, should be eaten in one bite; otherwise, cut the shrimp with your fork against the side of the dish.
- Toothpicks should not be used at the table, nor should food be picked from your teeth with your finger.
- Do *not* push back your plate when you are finished eating.
- Do not extend your pinky when drinking from a cup or glass.
- Don't put liquids in your mouth if you have food in it.
- When a finger bowl is served, dip your fingers into it, dry them on your napkin, and then place both the bowl and its doily on the table to the upper left of your plate.

Is Wine an Appurtenance of Class?

Wine collecting is meaningful, but only to a very small group of cognoscenti. The very special language of the wine connoisseur is sometimes daunting: "fresh, vigorous, with an appealing flowery bouquet and fullness of flavor," "full flavored, silky textured, eminently pleasing," "delicately dry, soft, romantic, and extremely delicious." Yet the differences in wines are not often that apparent. The taste is further complicated by the condition of one's digestive system on a specific day as well as the food served with the wine. A wine that was excellent with Monday's dinner may be quite disappointing with Tuesday's dinner.

One need not be a wine connoisseur to be able to taste the difference between a $2 bottle and a $5 bottle, but it may require a connoisseur to taste the difference between a $7.50 bottle and a $25 bottle. I came across a *New York Times* exposé dated October 14, 1982, headlined "Three Held after California Wine Is Sold As Top French." It seems that wine represented as one of France's most expensive and famous wines, Château Mouton-Rothschild, was being offered for sale at prices ranging from $250 to $400 per case; the genuine article is priced at $1,000 a case. But the only way the authorities could distinguish the French wine from the imitation was to make a chemical analysis! In contrast, it would require no chemical analysis to taste the difference between Mortimer's homemade ice cream and Haägen Dazs, or to taste the difference between the coffee served at the Palace Hotel in St. Moritz and the coffee made in your own home. You would recognize the superior quality of Mortimer's ice cream and the Palace Hotel's coffee even if you didn't like it.

Mimi and I were invited to the home of friends (he is a wine collector and connoisseur) for a formal dinner party. He asked us to come early to discuss the details of a three-week holiday trip we were taking together the following month. When we arrived, our friend said he was unhappy with the two cases of vintage Bordeaux he had just received. It had been intended for the evening's party. He wanted our opinion before sending it back, thinking he would serve instead a Bordeaux he already had in his wine cellar. I suggested that the four of us first make a blindfold test. The butler set it up. Three of us, his wife, Mimi and I preferred the wine he wanted to return. You might conclude that his taste buds were well-developed, but I would conclude that the next time around the score might have been reversed. We each had a fifty-fifty chance of being, should I say, right.

In many New York homes, wine has replaced alcohol as the preferred cocktail drink. A dry white wine, like a Chardonnay, is preferred to a German Moselle, which is relatively sweet. No one seems to want red wine for an aperitif. White wine is usually served with fish, veal, and chicken; red wine with red meat. Burgundy is stronger than Bordeaux, and, like Bordeaux, requires aging. Beaujolais, unlike Bordeau or Burgundy, should not be aged. Beaujolais is at its best in its first two years. Bordeaux and Burgundy should be opened a half hour before being served, to give the wine a chance to breathe. A wine bottle is always stored on its side so that the cork doesn't dry out.

Although being a connoisseur of wine may be considered one of the appurtenances of class, I believe that, in the final analysis, it really is much ado about nothing.

A Touch of Class at the Office

Unfortunately, gracious manners are no longer a hall-mark of business, and I sense a serious deterioration in even the smallest amenities. In a *New York Times* article, "Why Nobody Calls You Back Anymore," Robert K. Otterbourg, president of a public relations firm, said:

> We live in an on-line society that continually changes its many established business habits. Nowhere is this more evident than in the apparent deterioration in business manners. Good manners, in fact, seem no longer to exist as a sound administrative practice. Despite the overworked use of "Have a nice day," management seems to have taken a slightly less than chivalrous view toward what was once deemed accepted business behavior. To wit:
> —Letters sit for weeks on recipients' desks or go unanswered entirely.
> —Telephone calls, if returned, are returned long after the caller has fled elsewhere for help.
> —The telephone hold button is joyfully used to queue lists of callers.

I am often surprised by the fact that CEOs, many of whom have the advantages of a chauffeured limousine and, in some instances, a company plane, are not willing to pay for a really top-level secretary. This is quickly evident by failure to pass on messages, to return phone calls, to acknowledge letters received in the absence of the executive, etc. While it is true that good secretaries, like good people in general, are hard to find, they do exist and should have high priority on the executive list.

In my own business, I have made the training of thousands of employees from salesmen to designers to secretaries top priority, and have a certain sense of satisfaction that our company has a reputation for courtesy not only to our customers, but to all of the people our stores deal with. Yet, even in my own business, I am aware that something bad happens when a man becomes not just John Smith, but John Smith, Vice-President. A mantle of importance descends, and he goes from Jekyll to Hyde. He is apt to become difficult with his peers, a bully to underlings, obsequious to superiors and customers, and patronizing to the mailboy. An exaggeration? Perhaps, but it is commonplace and one reason these people advance no further. This lack of manners is found primarily in middle management. Too often there's a loss of even the most ordinary manners when people find themselves on the fast track.

Men and women at the very top in politics, the professions and business are almost always gracious. Charles Revson, the genius who created the Revlon cosmetic empire, was an exception. Revson was cruel, sarcastic and completely inconsiderate. Although he motivated his executives to a high performance level (with high pay), he also frequently suffered the loss of his most competent executives. As a result Revson had no one to take over for him when he learned about his terminal cancer. Revson was forced to reach out to ITT, Europe for a new chief executive, Michel Bergerac, who promptly changed the company's image with some unfortunate results.

In the hurly-burly of business, it might be said that the dropping of niceties is to be forgiven, and perhaps, even condoned, since the way to get ahead is to be strong and aggressive. But I would say just the opposite. The person with good manners—and by this I mean consideration for others—will have the edge in any situation and rise to the top faster than one who is rude.

So, here are a few reminders, culled from our own training program and my own observations for minding your business manners.

- Return phone calls as soon as possible. When your phone call is returned, say, "Thank you for returning my call."
- If the president or ranking officer of your company doesn't smoke, it would be good manners and good business not to smoke in his presence. The same would be true when spending time with a nonsmoking client.
- Four years ago we engaged the services of a man as vice-president of merchandising. He was not a smoker, but he did have the unfortunate habit of chewing gum. In all honesty, he was terribly discreet; but there it was, and I was not surprised to learn how many of us were annoyed by it. Chewing, like smoking, is a habit, but gum chewing is easier to break.
- Should you get a promotion or an award or anything else that advances your career, treat it quietly, very low key. Jealousy is a human trait, and you should do nothing to invite it. Throwing your weight around will transform a group of well-wishers into a group of people hoping to see you fail.
- Before leaving for lunch or any kind of meeting, take a

minute to wash your hands (sticky fingers and dirty fingernails are a turn-off), comb your hair, fix your necktie.

- Collect a small repertoire of interesting anecdotes, mainly light jokes. Off-color jokes will offend a certain number of people and also lower your class rating.
- Avoid arguments about politics and/or religion. It is better to lose an argument than to lose an account.
- Give thought to whom you will invite to a meeting. The presence of too many underlings may create the impression in clients or superiors that you can't handle the situation yourself, and clients don't always want an audience at a meeting.
- When attending meetings, don't grab someone else's usual seat. If there is no established seating, it's customary for senior executives to be seated first.
- If there are several people from your office calling on a client, it is certainly permissible for all to engage in conversation. If you are making a presentation, however, make sure you coordinate in advance who is going to say what and who is going to respond to which questions.
- Extend common courtesy to visitors. Stand up and greet anyone visiting you with an appointment. It is inconsiderate to keep visitors waiting in the reception room, unless absolutely necessary, in which case, advise them of the delay.
- Dress consistently, even if you do not have a meeting with a client. You should always be well turned out. It should not be necessary to dress up for important meetings. You should always feel that you look your best.
- What's important to someone else may not be important

to you, but consider the other person's feelings, and don't put off things that are easily and quickly taken care of.

• Patience is a virtue, but it's not always easy. It is desirable to praise people for their contributions to the overall pattern of business, no matter how small.

• Say please and thank you to everyone—your own office staff, clients and their employees.

• Office romances lead to wrack and ruin. There are *no* secrets.

• Be friendly but never intimate with office personnel, and avoid situations that could prove to be embarrassing (cocktails after work, candlelight dinners, etc.).

• When greeting a business acquaintance or upon being introduced, a firm handshake tells a lot about a person. Avoid a limp handshake. Actually feel the other person's hand and always, always look at him or her and smile. Nothing signals insecurity or shyness more than dropping the eyes or failing to smile when introduced.

• Be aware of your voice and don't be too loud. Control your temper.

• Don't gossip. The grapevine is usually the sour grapevine.

• When you read something nice about someone you know, drop him a note of congratulations.

• Favors are done all of the time in business, but don't forget a thank-you note.

• When criticism is called for, be sure the talk is private, between you and the other person, and certainly not in front of his peers.

• Be as courteous to salesmen as you are to a potential customer.

• It is customary for a man to remove his hat when riding

in an elevator with a woman. However, it is not necessary elsewhere in a building. There is frequent confusion in elevator etiquette about letting women off first. If the elevator is crowded, it is easier to leave in commonsense order.
• Be nice to the people on your way up, because you may meet the same people on your way down.

Tips for the Business Luncheons
• If you are the host, make every effort to arrive first at the luncheon. Whoever is first, be seated, but do not order wine or a cocktail or eat the bread until others arrive.
• It is customary to suggest a cocktail before the captain does. You would improve your own image, however, if you joined them with a glass of mineral water or clamato juice. Your clients may not be able to kick the habit themselves, but will think more highly of you if you have.
• Avoid dishes that may splash on your clothes, and skip the garlic.

And here is the only way to get a choice table in an "in" restaurant if you are not a regular. If you were the maitre d' or the proprietor of a very busy restaurant, you would hold your best tables for steady customers, for celebrities (who are good publicity) and for big tippers. So, if you want to be greeted warmly by the maitre d' and want to be seated at one of his best tables, you must fill one of the above requirements. However, let's suppose it's your first visit, and you still want a good table. Phone the maitre d' in advance and speak to him personally. Explain that you are entertaining an important client, that

"*Well, I'm glad to see that money still means something.*"
The best table—an appurtenance of class but not *the substance.*

you want the best table, and that it's worth $25, $15, $10, $5. Experience will teach you how much. Give him your name, your company, and say, "Mario, are you in a position to arrange this for me Tuesday night at eight-fifteen? Because if you can't I will have to go elsewhere. I am accustomed to the best, and I do *not* want to be embarrassed."

Will any one of the suggestions mentioned in this chapter earn you a ten rating on the class scale? Obviously not. However, each activity, by itself, is another step in the never-ending process of creating a fuller life.

5

---

*The Ultimate Test
of Class*

"You have to take the bitter with the better."
—*Gracie Allen*

YOU MAY HAVE NOTICED the serious thread running through many of my friends' comments about class earlier in this book:

"Class is caring about what is eternal . . ."
". . . a deep unpretentious nobility . . ."
". . . living without compromise."
". . . poise under pressure."
". . . perseverance in the face of the adversities of life. . ."

It took me a long while to understand that misery, loneliness, sickness, financial reverses, malicious gossip, shabby treatment by friends, the misfortune of children and duplicity of lovers are a normal part of life and should be expected to continue with varying degrees of severity. In childhood we are taught that young lovers marry and live happily ever after. As adults we probably never quite get that idea out of our head. As a result, every disappointment or misfortune may be felt as an unjustified and personal kick in the pants. But mishaps are the norm, and crises a commonplace. Accept them for what they are, a part of life's pattern, and life itself becomes more serene. Living is an act of faith, and only you can keep your life alive—"choked with laughter and choked with pain," as E. B. White wrote.

If your personal problems become overwhelming, you can put them into better perspective by involving yourself in group therapy. Your problems become easier to handle when you realize that a group of completely normal, gainfully employed adults have problems that are just as severe as yours.

Even if you don't need the therapy, you may want to consider joining a group for the additional insight it will give you into the realities and complexities of living. We have one friend, a very successful attorney, who believes that anyone who can afford it should visit a psychiatrist once a week in the same way that he opens each golf season with visits to his golf pro.

From time to time I receive a letter from a customer who, for one reason or another, is disappointed with our service or with our shirts. However, his distress couldn't be expressed more passionately if his indigestion had been diagnosed as cancer of the stomach. If a man's shirt problem is perceived as a tragedy, you may well imagine what the rest of his life is like. Such a man (unfortunately, in one way or another, they are legion) has lost perspective, and will probably wind up with an ulcer, high blood pressure, or both.

Along those lines, my own unhappy experiences with not one, but two Rolls-Royces, both seven-passenger limousines, made me realize that, regardless of label, one deals in the final analysis with people, and error is inevitable. I learned long ago to roll with the punches and have accepted Gracie Allen's advice to take "the bitter with the better." Dealing with adversity (real adversity) actually makes one stronger. There is a sense of accomplishment after one has handled an unhappy experience with grace.

When friends ask, "How do you feel?" I'm apt to answer, "My cup runneth over, but I am waiting for the ax to fall." Happily, the ax fell on Labor Day, September 6, 1982, at which time I was laid low by an extraordinarily severe attack of sciatica. I say happily because if it had happened on Memorial Day, it would have ruined my entire summer.

I was under the impression that sciatica could be cured by rubbing in Sloan's Liniment. Not so. I was taken to the hospital for X-rays. The orthopedist said "a little normal arthritis, nothing serious. After a few days' bed rest, you will be good as new." The sciatic nerve runs from the lower back down through the buttock, thigh, and leg, ending at the big toe. It is a nerve as sensitive as the nerve in a tooth. In my case, the excruciating pain was centered in my calf. I misunderstood the doctor's instructions and rented a wheelchair, thereby resting my leg as ordered. Unfortunately, the doctor had not made it clear to me that, although the pain was in my leg, the source of the pain was in my lower back. Sitting in a wheelchair made my condition worse, much worse. As a result, I was subsequently confined to my bed for seven weeks, four of them in traction. The only way to cure the swollen disc that was pressing on the sciatic nerve was to be in a horizontal position.

I had been waiting for the ax to fall. It fell, but I was completely prepared. It would seem unlikely that a person as active as I am would adjust to the inactivity resulting from seven weeks on my back. But I believed that I had had so much good luck that the bad luck was long overdue. That thinking permitted me to make the necessary adjustment to the pain, the painkillers and the lack of mobility. Pain or no pain, I kept quite busy with, among many other things, this book.

Should one of life's many problems get you down, sit down, and *think* about how to get yourself up. Don't fall into a state of helplessness or panic. Those who live life to its fullest marshal their energy and wits to fight their way through the rough times. Being prepared for disappointments equips one to handle them with a minimum of trauma. Lady Mendl's well-known quote: "Never complain, never explain" states it one way; I say it another with the phrase I have used to close my personal letters for the past twenty years, "Keep smiling."

George C. Scott, an actor famous for his stirring portrayals of General Patton in film and on stage as Shylock in Shakespeare's *Merchant of Venice*, admits that "having an appreciation of humor—about oneself and about life in general—is maybe the healthiest thing one can acquire, and I think I've moved in that direction. . . . I've begun to be more at peace with myself, less self-destructive. Just as critical, professionally, but maybe not so critical, personally. I don't get so angry anymore. I guess it comes from getting older, realizing really that life is very short and getting into a personal upset is counterproductive; it does you more damage than good."

Katharine Hepburn, in her seventies, reached a similar conclusion. "I've had certain things happen to me," she said in a recent interview, "that I was unable to view with a sense of humor at first, but I've struggled to, and I've discovered that the remarkable people I've known just seem to have that knack of being able to see things with a sense of humor. No matter what they are. It's part of our age. I think we're finally at a point where we've learned to see death with a sense of humor. I have to. When you're my age, it's like you're a car, and first a tire blows, and you get that fixed, and then a headlight goes, and you get that fixed. And then one day, you drive into a shop, and the man says, 'Sorry, Miss, they don't make these parts any more.' "

Every life has hundreds of unpleasant moments, some trivial, some tragic. How you handle these bad moments determines, to a great degree, your rating on the class scale. Here are two examples gained from personal experience:

It has been almost fifty years since I met my first wife, and we have remained friends. Anna has enormous energy and a steadfast belief in the soul of man. But 1978 proved to be cataclysmic. She was mugged twice, the second time suffering a broken leg. In March she was told she had lung cancer, and in April she underwent the necessary surgery. Her Christmas card for 1978 included a long series of cartoons illustrating a résumé of the year in verse:

A Christmas card in cartoon and verse from my first wife in which she pokes fun at disaster.

I've given the gate to '78.
There's hardly a date
I didn't hate in '78.

End faster, faster
I wished of that
disaster.

But wait—
One more look at '78.

Thanks to friends
     who in the clutches
Helped speed the
     end of the stinking crutches.

And listened while
     I sought to answer
Of how the hell
     You cope with cancer.

Of '78 I've had
     my fill
Of doctors, beds and
     being ill.

All that time
     the world kept going
Revolutions ebbing,
     flowing.

While from Michigan
To Carolina
Folks welcome
recognizing China,

Want an end to Shahs
and Boers,
Seek peace and freedom,
No more wars.

The jinx is past
I'm feeling fine.
A toast to the promise
of '79.

Women seem to handle adversity better than men. Women do come out fighting. I know half a dozen women who were widowed and at least six others whose husbands divorced them to marry someone younger. In each case, the unfortunate women immediately made themselves more attractive by acquiring new clothes, a new hairdo and new activities.

By contrast, men have a tendency to collapse when disaster strikes. But Jim Segal is one exception. Mimi and I met Jim and his Japanese wife, YoYo, in Morocco. We became fast friends though the Segals were twenty-five years younger. Jim had a brilliantly successful career in advertising. He then invested his savings in New Jersey real estate with sufficient success to go into partial retirement with YoYo and their two children on a large farm in the northern Catskills. It was there that he was struck down without warning by terminal cancer. He and YoYo dropped out of sight; he *refused* to let us visit. Eighteen months later an extraordinary letter arrived, reproduced in part below, which explained the disappearance and, more important, demonstrated one man's courage in the face of life's ultimate disappointment:

Dear Mimi and Mortimer,

Yes, the news of my death was premature. My demise, planned for September 1977, did not come off nearly as well as scheduled, to the not inconsiderable annoyance of my doctors.

So no: I am not in heaven, I'm in Houston. Where YoYo and I are alive and well and crazy in love. With each other. Still and even more so.

There's a reason we haven't been in touch with you, and I'd like to explain. Not so much by way of apology (though partly), but because I think it's kind of interesting.

You know how when you're a kid you learn that Bambi's father, the Great Stag of the Forest, goes off into the woods to die by himself. When you're in college you learn the same thing, only they call it cultural anthropology. When an old Eskimo lady loses her teeth and can't chew on hide to soften it for clothing, she goes off from the village to die alone is arctic isolation. Nathanael West used to say that people went to L.A. to die, in the same kind of way!

Well it's really like that. When I was scheduled to die, YoYo and I kind of went off by ourselves; we retreated into psychic isolation. No calls, no dinner invitations, no cocktail parties, no public facade. You retreat from the world, you try to gather yourself together, you pack your gear, you get ready for transit.

Only I never tripped out. I don't know what happened and I don't really know what's happening now. . . .

I am not cured; I am not in remission; I am not normal, not healthy, not well; but neither am I dying. I am a lot of nots, and no ams. I have a case of terminal limbo. It's kind of spooky, and I enter hospitals now with the same spookiness that I used to enter movie theaters to see Dracula and Wolfman movies when I was a kid. I knew they weren't for real—but I was nervous and scared anyway.

Lots of things have happened, on different levels of our lives. We sold the farm. It was a gorgeous fantasy life that didn't seem to be fun anymore. More than that, we wanted to marshal our assets for the long haul, for estate planning. ("Get your papers in order," the doctor had said.) That was his euphemism when he first told me I was dying. I hadn't understood. Would you? My mind just couldn't or wouldn't comprehend his damned delicacy. I thought he wanted me to sign some hospital papers, releases, waivers, something, anything. Huh? I'd said. You know, your papers, he'd said. What papers, I'd said, and then, slowly dawning over me, I said, you mean my will? And he'd smiled very gently and benevolently, like James Mason in *Heaven Can Wait*, and I'd hated him for his gentility and indirectness and subtlety, and I suppose mostly for his news.

Anyhow—we moved to Houston. Bought a townhouse. Settled down, settled in. Began a new—may I say it?—life. . . .

There's no pretty ribbon to wrap it all neatly in, but

I've turned Jack Benny's age now—39—and at this strange threshold of my life I feel—simply happy. There's so much I've done and gone through; and I feel good and proud to have done it, made it, seen it, felt it, been through it. There's still so much ahead I want to know and touch and feel and understand. I still feel so much potential ahead of me. I want to live so much! Lord, how I'd hate to die now, especially now. Yet—can you understand what I'm driving at—if I died today, I'd die, not content, but happy.

We are coming out of our shell; we are metamorphosizing out of our cocoon; we are rejoining the living; and we extend our hands to you in affection and in hopes of renewing what we view and value as an odd, offbeat, and unusual friendship. . . .

Jim

In 1979 I was the associate producer of a Broadway comedy called *Checking Out*, written by, directed by and starring Allen Swift. He played the role of an old *bon vivant* who had once been the leading star of New York's Yiddish Theater. At the time the play opens, Swift has sent telegrams to his four grown children inviting them to a gala party celebrating his eighty-first birthday. It was to be a luxurious affair for his family and many friends, after which he intended to check out—arrange his own death by suicide. He had lived his life in great style, and he wanted to die in style without enduring the debilitating effects of a stroke, heart attack, terminal cancer or senility. His children were horrified, and insisted that a fulltime, live-in nurse be retained to prevent him from taking his own life. When he refused to listen to reason, they said they would commit him to an insane asylum. He was thus forced to accept a live-in nurse. How he outwitted the nurse and his four adult children makes for a very funny and moving play.

I keep a death list of friends, acquaintances, relatives, and certain public personalities with whom I have identified. Having a death list sounds morbid, I know, but whenever I add a new name, I glance through the list and am reminded of the many happy occasions I shared with those now gone, experiences that certainly enriched my life. In that way, those on my death list continue to live. And it makes me feel better to know that in the same way I will continue to live in the memories of others after I too am gone.

As one grows older, it becomes obvious that other people look younger, but what is not so obvious is that although you look older, you don't feel older and are still capable of childish behavior. It becomes hard to understand that people see you differently than you see yourself. I have been receiving compliments for years on how young I look so you can imagine my surprise when one summer night, about ten years ago, while Mimi was visiting her mother in Hollywood, I went to the movies. I said, "One, please." The cashier said, "Is that a senior citizen?" I asked her how old that would be, assuming it was fifty-five years, and she said, "Sixty-five," to which I said, "Yes, please," without further comment. The passage of my own life is written on the aging faces of my friends, and, evidently, on my own face as well.

In the beginning my life moved very slowly. The older I got the faster it moved, and in recent years my life has

Did I say that the passage of my own life is written on the aging faces of my friends??!! The author at sixty-five.

actually been racing. The years seem to go by with the speed of months. Under the circumstances, it is to be expected that my mind turns to the subject of dying.

Death may be seen as the ultimate disappointment that life holds in store and the one that perhaps tests our mettle and our rating on the class scale more than any other. But I feel that the act of dying is actually the ultimate *adventure* in the act of living. Ever since that thought occurred to me, the thought of dying has ceased to terrify me. Instead of the horror of helplessly watching someone else die, you will go through the experience of acting it out (actually living through it) yourself.

In preparation, I have built a granite sarcophagus for two—one side for me, the other side for Mimi. There being no family crest, I had the Custom Shop logo carved into each of the four corners. To complete my preparations I made a will and wrote my own epitaph, "Levitt was no stuffed shirt."

Keep smiling!

MORTIMER LEVITT

is a self-made millionaire who has seen and done just
about everything. He has produced plays, films, and
television features, and is involved in many cultural
and philanthropic activities: a board member of
Lincoln Center's Film Society; founder-owner of
the Mortimer Levitt Gallery, 1943–1955; a founding member and producer at both the Manhattan
Theater Club and the Levitt Pavilion in Westport,
Connecticut; board chairman of Young Concert
Artists; and former board chairman of Daytop
Village's drug rehabilitation centers. Last, but not
least, Levitt is the founder and sole owner of The
Custom Shop, Shirtmakers, with some fifty-nine
stores coast to coast, a business from which he says,
"they will have to carry me out feet first." Now in
his seventy-eighth year, Levitt remains an active
skier, sailor, pianist, and tennis player (singles only).